GROVE PRESS MODERN DRAMATISTS

Grove Press Modern Dramatists

Series Editors: *Bruce King* and *Adele King*

Published titles

Neil Carson, *Arthur Miller*

Ruby Cohn, *New American Dramatists, 1960–1980*

Bernard F. Dukore, *Harold Pinter*

Julian Hilton, *Georg Büchner*

Leonard C. Pronko, *Eugène Labiche and Georges Feydeau*

Theodore Shank, *American Alternative Theater*

Further titles in preparation

GROVE PRESS MODERN DRAMATISTS

ARTHUR MILLER

by **Neil Carson**

Associate Professor of English
University of Guelph, Canada

Grove Press, Inc., New York

First published 1982 by The Macmillan Press Ltd.,
London and Basingstoke.

First Evergreen Edition 1982
First Printing 1982
ISBN: 0–394–17966–8
Library of Congress Catalog Card Number: 81–84704

Printed in Hong Kong

GROVE PRESS, INC., 196 West Houston Street, New York, N.Y. 10014

Contents

List of Plates

Editors' Preface

The *Grove Press Modern Dramatists* is an international series of introductions to major and significant nineteenth and twentieth century dramatists, movements and new forms of drama in Europe, Great Britain, America and new nations such as Nigeria and Trinidad. Besides new studies of great and influential dramatists of the past, the series includes volumes on contemporary authors, recent trends in the theatre and on many dramatists, such as writers of farce, who have created theatre 'classics' while being neglected by literary criticism. The volumes in the series devoted to individual dramatists include a biography, a survey of the plays, and detailed analysis of the most significant plays, along with discussion, where relevant, of the political, social, historical and theatrical context. The authors of the volumes, who are involved with theatre as playwrights, directors, actors, teachers and critics, are concerned with the plays as theatre and discuss such matters as performance, character interpretation and staging, along with themes and contexts.

Editors' Preface

Grove Press Modern Dramatists are written for people interested in modern theatre who prefer concise, intelligent studies of drama and dramatists, without jargon and an excess of footnotes.

BRUCE KING
ADELE KING

FOR EDWINA

1
The Young Playwright (1915-49)

Arthur Miller is one of the three or four leading playwrights of the American theatre. While his position in the history of American (and indeed world) drama is assured, it may be many years before there is general agreement about the nature of his contribution and the order in which his plays should be ranked. For not only is the playwright still active, but there is at the heart of his work something which seems to perplex and divide his critics. Some dismiss him as little more than a disciple of Ibsen; others cite him as a penetrating critic of American society and an important innovator in the theatre. Some critics call his work 'blood-less', while others admire the subtlety of his characterisation. There is disagreement, too, about whether Miller's dramatic vision is profound or superficial, clear-eyed or sentimental.

Closely related to Miller's uncertain critical reputation is his paradoxical position in the theatre. While European productions of his plays appear to be gaining in popularity – the National Theatre of Great Britain's production of

1

Death of a Salesman was a hit of the 1979–80 season – American audiences seem to find his plays less exciting than they once did. This reaction may be due to New York's belated discovery of modernism in the experimental theatre movement of the 1960s and 70s. But it also reflects the difficulty of the serious American playwright to find a sympathetic audience in the current theatrical climate. The Broadway of the 1940s was prosperous and flexible enough to accommodate both the best and the worst of dramatic art. As production costs have increased year by year, however, it has become more and more difficult for anything but light entertainment to survive there. Instead of the mass audience for which Miller has always written, Broadway now caters to that narrow stratum of society that can afford to pay $25 to $30 per ticket. It is Miller's misfortune to be a serious populist dramatist at a time when entertainment and 'seriousness' have come to seem incompatible. Consequently he is regarded as naive and old-fashioned by the intellectuals, and rather solemn and moralistic by the popular press.

The difficulty in arriving at some kind of balanced judgement of the dramatist is that there is some truth in both these views. Compared to a Beckett or a Sartre, Miller seems naively hopeful; beside the formal experiments of an Ionesco, Miller's carefully crafted plays look a little musty. There *is* a certain preachy quality in some of his plays that tends to make some audiences or readers uncomfortable. It is extraordinarily difficult, therefore, to respond to Miller's plays on all levels at once, to give full weight to the ironies, ambiguities and ambivalences, as well as to the seemingly confident assertions and the apparently simplistic generalisations.

Another problem with the plays is their acknowledged autobiographical nature. Although most of the dramas are based on an external source (overheard story, novel, published memoir), they become translated in the course of composition into something personal. 'The writer who wants to describe life', Miller once explained, 'must describe his own experiences.'[1] Going even further, he maintained that the 'best work that anybody ever writes is the work that is on the verge of embarrassing him . . . . Where he puts himself on the line.'[2] Miller's natural tendency in the direction of subjectivism is compounded by his particular talent. Whereas writers like Dickens or Shakespeare appear, like photographic plates, to be able to reproduce the astonishing variety of nature, Miller is more like a painter who works always from the same model. He does not so much create other people in his plays as divide himself up into a number of *personae*.

It is the amalgam of the documentary and the personal in the plays that presents the reader or spectator with the most difficult challenge. Many critics find that the autobiographical elements in some of the plays give them a heightened intensity and psychological reality. Others sense in the personal preoccupations of the playwright an inability (or at least a failure) to enter sympathetically into the lives and problems of characters very different from his own.

Arthur Miller was born on 17 October 1915 in New York City and lived the first fourteen years of his life in Harlem. That section of the city was then a fairly prosperous middle-class area of mixed ethnic composition, and the playwright remembers the time as one of relative innocence – of evenings spent around the piano singing the latest hit songs, of winters skating on Central Park, of summers playing baseball on litter-free streets with no garbage cans. The Miller family was fairly typical. Isidore had come to America from Austria with his parents when he was still quite young and had worked his way up to become a successful manufacturer of ladies' coats. His wife, Augusta, a first-generation American born in New York, had taught public school before her marriage. Although not orthodox, the Millers could speak Yiddish, observed Jewish customs, and gave their children a fairly sound background in Judaism.

In 1929 the family moved to the Midwood section of Brooklyn, then a semi-rural suburb of New York City with great elm trees, unpaved roads and empty spaces behind the houses. The move was occasioned in part by a slackening in the Miller business, but perhaps as much by Mrs Miller's desire to be close to her relatives who had moved to that area following the First World War. Here the family lived for long periods with Mrs Miller's father and, as the playwright recalls, about thirty uncles who were always in and out of the house. In the summer, Arthur and his cousins fished off the rocks of Coney Island, and the family kept a vegetable garden as well as rabbits and chickens to reduce the number of journeys to the grocery store four miles away. After the collapse of the stock market which destroyed the Miller business, the gardening became more than a convenience.

The 'crash' of 1929 and the Depression which followed it were the major influences on the playwright's slowly developing view of life. Not only did they come close to destroying his father, who never completely recovered his financial position, but they put serious strains on the young Miller's relationship with other members of his family. The relative poverty to which they had been reduced meant that sacrifices were called for and every desire to place self-realisation above family solidarity implied a fundamental betrayal. Even more profoundly the failure of the econo-

4

mic system called into question everything that young Arthur had seen or learned up to that time. The promise had been fake. The 'reality' was not the chauffeured limousines of Harlem, but the breadlines of New York and the man fainting from hunger on a back porch in Brooklyn. Miller became convinced that there was an invisible world behind the apparent one, and he began to search for the hidden laws that would explain this catastrophe.[3]

When he graduated from high school in 1932, he found that his academic record was not good enough to get him into university and, in any case, there was no money to send him. He worked at a variety of jobs until he settled down as a shipping clerk in an automobile-parts warehouse in Manhattan at $15 a week. It was there that he discovered serious literature. In his year at the warehouse he read more than he had in the rest of his life. He was drawn to the great Russian novelists, especially Dostoievsky, and he began to dream of becoming a writer.

In 1934 Miller applied to the University of Michigan requesting special consideration of his case and was granted conditional admission. Not daring to admit that he wanted to become a serious writer, he enrolled in journalism and became a night editor on the student paper. At university he began to widen his political perspectives. He became interested in the Spanish Civil War, and found himself increasingly attracted to the socialist ideals of the time. Along with most of his idealistic contemporaries he became convinced of the need for change and progress in society; he believed passionately that what he thought mattered, and that he and his friends could have an effect upon events.[4]

In the March break of his second year at Michigan, Miller tried for one of the annual Hopwood literary prizes. Avery Hopwood had been a successful playwright, author of such American classics as *Getting Gertie's Garter*, and *Up in Mabel's Room*, who had bequeathed some $300,000 to the University of Michigan to establish annual awards for drama, fiction, poetry and the essay. Miller had attended the theatre once or twice only, and had never written a play; nevertheless he resolved to submit a drama to the judges, and accordingly spent six days writing *No Villain*. Some three months later he was awarded the first prize of $250 and his playwriting career had begun.

No Villain is the story of a Jewish family living in the suburbs of New York, and of the crisis brought on by a strike which threatens to destroy their garment business. The head of the household, Abe Simon, is an ambitious but narrow businessman who has alienated his wife Esther by his long hours at the shop and by his resentment of Esther's eighty-year-old father who is living with them. The children, two sons and a daughter, are caught in the middle of this antagonism. Ben, the oldest, is working for his father while Arnie is studying at the University of Michigan. The tensions in the family are brought to a head when Arnie returns to New York for the summer holidays. Against the opposition of Ben, who does not want to see his brother trapped as he is, Abe persuades his younger son to help out at the shop. In the course of his first day he is beaten up when he unknowingly tries to cross a picket line. Angered by his father's attempt to deceive him, he declares his allegiance to the strikers. Feeling abandoned by one son and fearing bankruptcy, Abe pleads with Ben, who reluctantly agrees, to marry the daughter of a wealthy manufacturer and thereby save the family fortunes. At a meeting of the Manufacturers' Association, a resolution approving the hiring of strikebreakers is passed over Abe's and Ben's objections. At home Arnie tries to persuade Ben to break off his engagement and abandon the shop in order to join the right side in the struggle. When they overhear the grandfather offering to help Abe, Ben is ashamed and the sons quarrel. Their animosity is quelled, however, when the grandfather dies of a heart attack. The third act shows the final collapse of the business and the beginning of a reconciliation between Abe and Esther. Ben breaks his engagement of convenience, and with new-found confidence declares his intention of making his own way in the world.

The play is naive and melodramatic, but it is interesting as an anticipation of situations and themes that will become central to Miller's later drama. Characteristically, it is a realistic treatment of a domestic crisis which is precipitated by external, political events. The conflicts provoked arise from what might be called ideological differences, but these are by no means confined to political ideologies. They include opposing views on class warfare, but they also number among them different attitudes towards loyalty, self-sacrifice and love. At the core they are concerned with the problem of reconciling selfish and generous impulses, and of living humanely. In the end, every member of the family comes to realise that there are higher values than monetary ones and a larger world than that circumscribed by the household walls.

Considerably encouraged by his success, Miller transferred out of journalism into English and enrolled in the playwriting course offered by Professor Kenneth Rowe. In Rowe's classes Miller was introduced to the dramatic forms of the past, especially the realistic works of the Norwegian playwright Henrik Ibsen. Through close analysis of plays such as *A Doll's House*, Rowe showed how each development in the well-constructed plot was an organic growth from character and situation. Rowe particularly admired Ibsen's emphasis on social problems and the way

7

in which the playwright focused on the questions of moral values, integrity and will underlying those problems. Rowe's strict ideas about the process of playwriting were to influence the way in which Miller approached his craft. For Rowe, the impulse to write a play entirely out of oneself was a sign of weakness or of the slackening of dramatic imagination and should be sternly suppressed. The better method was to begin with a good plot. 'It makes no difference what [that plot] is or where [the author] finds it,' he wrote. 'Let him present the story, translate it, if necessary, in terms of a background and kind of people he knows and understands. Then let him develop the play earnestly and sincerely in truth to the characters and to life as he sees it.'[5]

During his first year in Rowe's class, Miller revised *No Villain* which, under the title *They Too Arise*, was awarded a $1250 award by the Theatre Guild's Bureau of New Plays and was produced in Ann Arbor and Detroit. He also wrote his second play, *Honors at Dawn*, which in June won him his second Hopwood Award. *Honors* is another strike play, much more conventionally leftist than *No Villain*, which tells of a young idealist who becomes disillusioned with the corruption and duplicity of the university where he is enrolled as a student. When he discovers that his brother has been paid by the university administration to spy on campus radicals, he leaves to join a labour union. There he finds a new sense of commitment as well as a feeling of personal integrity and social responsibility.

In his final year Miller completed a third play, *The Great Disobedience*, but it failed to win the Hopwood Award, which went instead to a work by his close friend, Norman Rosten. When he graduated in 1938, therefore, it was with a slightly more realistic knowledge of the difficulties that lay ahead of him in his chosen career. Success on Broadway was to come more slowly than it had in the friendly atmosphere of the University of Michigan. Laying siege to the Great White Way was a long-term project and Miller's immediate concern in the spring of 1938 was to support himself while he continued to write. To this end he joined the Federal Theatre Project, a government-sponsored relief agency established to provide work for actors, writers and theatre technicans. With fellow graduate, Norman Rosten, he worked on *Listen My Children*, a rather crude left-wing comedy to which he contributed a one-act sketch based on his experiences collecting relief payments. In June of 1939, troubled by reports of communist influence in the Federal Theatre, Congress refused to renew its appropriation for the Project. That put an end to Miller's $22.77-a-week salary, and was his introduction to the methods and influence of the recently formed House Committee on Un-American Activities.

(ii)

With the demise of the Federal Theatre Project, Miller turned his hand to a variety of jobs while he continued to write. Unable to join the armed service because of a knee injury sustained in high school, he went to work in the Brooklyn Navy Yard. He also married; his bride, Mary Slattery, was a girl he had met at university. She was Catholic, the daughter of an Ohio insurance salesman, and as idealistic, high-principled and emotionally inhibited as Miller himself. The young couple lived in Brooklyn, and Mary went to work as a secretary in a publishing house to contribute to the family income.

Slowly Miller began to establish himself as a writer for radio, but he found the medium restricting and continued to dream of conquering Broadway. After *Listen My Children* he wrote four or five plays, none of which satisfied him. Then he heard the story of a businessman from the Middle West whose financial success led him first to believe that everyone was trying to rob him, and finally to commit suicide. He worked on a dramatic version of the story for several months, but had difficulty in giving it the form he felt it needed. The play was published by Edwin Seaver in an anthology of new American writing entitled *Cross-Section*, and then accepted for production by Herbert H. Harris. *The Man Who Had All the Luck*, as the play was called, was directed by Joseph Field as a folk comedy, rather than as the serious drama Miller thought it to be. It opened on 23 November 1944, received bad reviews, and closed after four performances. The production won a Theatre Guild Award for the author, and attracted the attention of such producers as Harold Clurman who expressed an interest in future work. Most important of all, however, it stimulated Miller to analyse the reasons for his failure.

A major problem in rehearsals had been the time-consuming scene changes necessitated by the script. Miller had called for four highly realistic locations including a mechanic's shop with a car on stage. These requirements had been determined in part by the structure of the play. Miller had written the work in a straightforward narrative covering a period of about three years during which time the protagonist got married, prospered and had a child. Because all of the action was shown, there was very little emphasis on events before the curtain went up, and less exploration of the relationship between past actions and present consequences. Indeed, the whole process of cause and effect was subverted in this play because of Miller's very heavy reliance on coincidence. The result is that there is little attention paid to the relationship between man and society. The playwright himself recognised that he had been betrayed by what he called 'wonder'. By this he meant that he had allowed himself to deal with the metaphysical questions in the play directly instead of letting them arise out of a more 'realistic' story. He resolved in his next play to create a greater illusion of life, and to approach the unseen only through the concretely visualised.

During these years Miller also began to broaden his range as a writer. *Situation Normal* (1944), a book of reportage based on interviews with American servicemen in various placement centres across the country, illustrates Miller's tendency to combine a sharp eye for realistic detail with a predeliction for the hasty generalisation or the apt admonishment. *Focus* (1945), a novel, is the first of Miller's published works to deal explicitly with his own Jewish experience. It treats anti-Semitism from the point of view of a non-Jew who suddenly encounters the effects of prejudice because of the alteration in his appearance when he begins to wear glasses. Lawrence Newman's indignation at being arbitrarily 'degraded' in this way makes him stand up to the attacks of the fascist Christian Front and assert his common humanity with the Jews. Both of these works mark new advances for Miller, but they were taking him in the wrong direction.

In 1945 a visiting relative told him the story of a girl who denounced her father when she discovered that he had been supplying defective engine-parts to the Army. Once again Miller's imagination was captured by an incident that both fascinated and puzzled him. During the next two years he sought a way to embody the theme in dramatic action. As a result of the failure of his first play Miller was determined to avoid what he had come to regard as the weaknesses of that work. This time he resolved not to express any idea unless it was literally forced out of a character's mouth. The result was a tightly crafted realistic play similar in structure to his undergraduate work but quite unlike the plays he had been writing since graduation. The finished script, called *All My Sons*, was picked up by producers Harold Clurman, Elia Kazan and Walter Fried. The play opened at the Coronet Theatre on 29 January 1947 and ran for 328 performances. It won the Drama Critics' Circle Award, was produced in Paris and Stockholm and made into a film.

With the money he made from *All My Sons* Miller began to consolidate his life. He bought a house in Brooklyn and a farm in Roxbury, Connecticut. One of his first tasks on his new farm was to build a split-shingle cabin in which he could seclude himself to write. In this cabin during 1947–8 he began a love story about working people in an industrial city which he called *Plenty Good Times*. The play did not develop easily, however, and one evening Miller began thinking about a salesman he had known when he had worked for his father. Gradually he found his imagination flooded by images of this man. He worked feverishly through the night, and in the morning had finished two thirds of a play which he called *The Inside of His Head*, The final third of the play proved more difficult, and it was some three months before he completed the manuscript and sent it off to a producer. Walter Fried (who had been co-producer of *All My Sons*) and Kermit Bloomgarden agreed to accept it immediately and they succeeded in getting Kazan as director and Jo Mielziner as designer.

In September, Mielziner proposed to solve the scenic problems posed by the script by using a single suggestive setting of the salesman's house, and playing all other scenes on various areas of the forestage. The plan involved building an addition over several rows of seats in the Morosco Theatre, and would require considerable rewriting on the part of the author to integrate the action into the proposed setting. By December this rewriting had been completed and rehearsals began.[6] Now called *Death of a Salesman*, the play opened in Philadelphia in January 1949, and moved to New York the following month.

The success of *Salesman* transformed Miller's life. The play ran on Broadway for 742 performances, won the Pulitzer Prize, the Antoinette Perry Award and the Drama Critics' Award. It earned its author royalties amounting to about $160,000 a year from the New York production, and an equal amount from two or three touring companies. Furthermore, it elevated Miller to a position of prominence where he became exposed to both adulation and criticism of a kind he had not previously experienced. After more than ten years of struggling to establish himself as a playwright, such success was heady. But it was also treacherously seductive.

2
Looking for the World that would be Perfect

During the 1940s the Millers had lived in relative obscurity, and it had been a simple matter to separate their private and professional lives. Of necessity they had existed quietly, and the demands of their two young children, Jane Ellen (born 1944) and Robert (born 1946), occupied much of their energy and attention. The religious and temperamental differences between Mary and her mother-in-law, and the fact that the children were being raised without a sense of their Jewish background, imposed slight but perceptible strains on family relationships. But these problems seemed minor, and the Roxbury farm enabled the young couple to secure some privacy and independence. In the next five years all that would change. As one of the New York stage's most exciting new talents, Miller found himself drawn more and more into the public spotlight. There his outspoken opposition to political persecution and his sympathy for leftist causes brought him unfavourable attention from right-wing commentators and the unwelcome attention of the House Committee on

Un-American Activities.

Originally created in 1938 as a special (that is, not permanent) committee to investigate the extent of communist infiltration into American life, the House Committee on Un-American Activities had been disbanded during the war. In 1945, however, it was revived as a standing committee, and its authority was considerably strengthened three years later as a result of its role in the Alger Hiss case. Hiss was a high-ranking official in the State Department who was accused by Whittaker Chambers of being a communist agent. Hiss vigorously denied the charges, but subsequent investigation established that he had perjured himself and that in all probability he had at some time been acting as a Soviet spy. The exposure of an international network of espionage reaching into the very heart of the State Department shocked and horrified Americans, most of whom were ready to back the efforts of the House Committee on Un-American Activities to unearth more information about such a threat to the national security.

Even among its opponents, the real danger of the House Committee on Un-American Activities was not its declared purpose of searching out enemies of the state, but the extra-legal means it employed to pursue these ends. Since witnesses before the Committee hearings were not technically accused of anything, they were provided with none of the safeguards designed to protect witnesses in a court of law. They could consult with lawyers, but their counsel could not speak on their behalf. There was no provision made for cross-examination, so hearsay, prejudice and allegation became part of the official record. Furthermore, far from protecting the identity of witnesses, the House Committee on Un-American Activities did all it could to publicise its hearings so that 'unfriendly' witnesses could be exposed to an increasingly hysterical public opinion. Refusals to answer questions by pleading the First or Fifth Amendments of the Constitution were generally considered to be admissions of guilt, and the unlucky witnesses might face ostracism by their friends, dismissal from their jobs, or even physical violence. Innumerable careers were damaged or destroyed by Committee investigations and more than a dozen suicides have been linked to appearances, or subpoenas to appear, before the House Committee on Un-American Activities.

During the first half of the 1950s Miller's own political beliefs and the concerns he expressed in his plays brought him more and more directly into opposition with the House Committee on Un-American Activities. Late in 1950 his adaptation of Henrik Ibsen's *An Enemy of the People* opened at the Broadhurst Theatre in New York for a short run. It told the story of a Norwegian officer of health who is ostracised by his community when he threatens to publicise the fact that the town's lucrative health spa is polluted. The play was generally perceived as criticism of the persecution of liberals and intellectuals by conservative public opinion (with the implication that truth is on the side of the minority). What earned Miller the lasting enmity of the Committee however, was the appearance of *The Crucible* in 1953.

Miller had been fascinated by the story of the seventeenth-century witches of Salem ever since he first read about them at university. He was struck by the 'terrible marvel' of people who 'could have such a belief in themselves and in the rightness of their consciences [that they would] give up their lives rather than say what they thought was false'.[7] And if the courage of the 'witches' provided an inspiration for the present age, the conduct of the judges might also illustrate something about universal

16

human nature. Miller 'wanted to tell people what had happened before and where to find the early underlying forces of such a phenomenon'.[8]

The Crucible opened in New York on 22 January, 1953 at the Martin Beck Theatre. It ran for 197 performances and won the Antoinette Perry and Donaldson awards as the most distinguished American drama of the year. Critical response of both audiences and journalists was mixed. It was probably inevitable, given the atmosphere of the times, that most people would see in *The Crucible* a thinly disguised attack on the investigations of the House Committee and by implication a plea of innocence for all of its victims. The play was coldly received by its opening-night audience, and Miller began to find the world a less friendly place than it had been after *Salesman*.

Miller's next Broadway show opened more than two years later on 29 September 1955. It was a double bill at the Coronet Theatre made up of two short plays, *A View from the Bridge* and *A Memory of Two Mondays*. The plays had been written in response to a request from Martin Ritt and a group of actors appearing in Clifford Odets's *The Flowering Peach*. The production was doing poor business at the time, and the actors wanted a one-act play they could perform before an invited audience. Miller completed the plays in a little under four weeks, but by that time *The Flowering Peach* had closed, and it was decided to give them a full Broadway production. Written originally for intimate and informal performance, the plays represented something of a new departure for the author. Of the two, *A View from the Bridge* is the more interesting since Miller later expanded it into a full-length play. The story, which Miller had heard some years earlier from a waterfront worker, was one he could not get out of his mind. He felt that he 'could not fit it into himself' and he wrote the play to 'see what it might mean'.[9] If *View* is about people and incidents remote from his own experience, *A Memory of Two Mondays* is a dramatic reminiscence of his own youth. The play is a delicate study of the scarcely changing rhythms of life in industrial society. Set in an automobile-parts warehouse in Manhattan, it tells of the resolve of one of the young workers, Bert, to go to college, and of his final departure from the shipping room. The drama unfolds without comment or significant climax, but it records the difference between the undirected lives of the majority and the self-determining will of the young Bert. The two plays received cool reviews, and ran a disappointing 149 performances.

About this time Miller began working on a film which was to record the work of the Youth Board of New York City, an agency which was attempting to reach and rehabilitate members of the violent Manhattan street gangs. During the summer of 1955 he began spending his evenings on the New York streets visiting juvenile gangs with workers from the Youth Board, and prepared a twenty-five-page scenario for the film, which he proposed calling *Bridge to a Savage World*. When news of Miller's involvement with the project spread, however, questions began to be asked about the propriety of spending public funds to hire a writer with known socialist sympathies. An attack against Miller was launched in the *New York World-Telegram,* and in the next few months it was joined by editorial writers, the American Legion and other patriotic organisations. It also seems that members of the House Committee on Un-American Activities suggested to the Youth Board that it should sever its relationship with the playwright. In spite of Miller's express denial that he was a communist, the Youth Board finally voted in December to drop the project which by then had brought them too much unwelcome publicity.

Miller might reasonably have thought by the end of 1955 that he had experienced the worst the House Committee on Un-American Activities could do to him. In the following spring, however, using Miller's application for a passport as an excuse, the Committee subpoenaed the dramatist as a witness, ostensibly to help them with their investigation into the illegal use of passports. Miller travelled to Washington where, in response to questions that had little to do with passports, he repeated his denials of having ever belonged to the Communist Party, and refused to give the names of individuals (already known to the Committee) whom he had seen at a communist writers' meeting in 1947. As a result of this refusal, Miller was cited for contempt of Congress, and his case was brought before the House on 15 February, 1957. In his defense, Miller's lawyers pointed out that the case against the playwright appeared to be vindictive since some thirteen individuals, most of them in more sensitive positions than Miller, had also refused to name associates known to be communists, and yet not one of those individuals had been cited for contempt. After a relatively short debate in which only some half-dozen congressmen spoke in defence of the dramatist, Congress voted overwhelmingly against Miller. On 19 July he was fined $500 and given a one-month suspended sentence. He appealed the case to the Supreme Court and a year later, on 7 August 1958, he was acquitted.

(i)

In retrospect it seems almost certain that the decision of the House Committee on Un-American Activities to subpoena Miller had more to do with the playwright's publicity value than with his knowledge of a communist conspiracy. As a successful Broadway celebrity, Miller had considerable news value in his own right, but about this time rumours were beginning to circulate linking his name romantically with that of the even more newsworthy Marilyn Monroe. Miller's marriage, which had been slowly disintegrating over the past few years, finally ended in a Reno divorce in June 1956. About the same time Miss Monroe was winning a divorce from her husband Joe DiMaggio, the famous baseball player. The couple were seen together in public, but it was not until after Miller's appearance in Washington that the stories were confirmed. In an attempt to win some privacy for themselves, they scheduled a press conference at Miller's Roxbury farm. Some 400 journalists and photographers representing newspapers from all over the world flocked to the country to get news of what was to become one of the most publicised matches of the decade.

There is no doubt that much of the curiosity surrounding the romance was stimulated by the apparent incongruities of the union. At forty-one, Miller was being hailed as America's leading playwright, and was generally regarded as a serious (even solemn) intellectual. Monroe, some eleven years his junior, was the Hollywood sex symbol of her day, a woman of extraordinary and luminous beauty, but of as yet unproven intellectual endowments. To many the relationship seemed like a charming fairy tale; to others it was an astonishing misalliance. Rumours of the liaison between the playwright and the actress first became widespread in 1955, but their relationship had begun some years earlier. They first met in Hollywood in 1950 when Miller was on the coast with Elia Kazan trying to arrange the financing for a film about the New York waterfront. Kazan introduced them, and they were immediately attracted to one another. From internal evidence in the plays, it is highly likely that Miller told his wife about his meeting with Marilyn, and that this further complicated a relationship that was already beginning to fray. Miller's personal problems at this time began to be reflected in his work, especially in the studies of strained marriages that appear in *The Crucible* and the revised version of *A View from the Bridge.*

It is entirely probable that the Miller marriage would have ended in divorce in any case, but the process was accelerated in the spring of 1955 when Marilyn Monroe arrived in New York. Tired of being exploited by her studio, the actress had formed her own company, moved to the east and begun taking serious acting classes with Lee Strasberg at the Actors' Studio. Miller began seeing her again at the homes of mutual friends, and by the end of the year the romance had been revived. Convinced that no reconciliation with his wife was possible, he spent six weeks in a rented shack at Pyramid Lake fifty miles northeast of Reno in order to qualify for a Nevada divorce. On 11 June 1956, he finally obtained his divorce from Mary Slattery and seventeen days later married Marilyn Monroe in a civil ceremony in a court house in Westchester County. Two days later, the couple were married again in a Jewish ceremony at the home of friends. Following the wedding, the couple moved into a luxurious apartment on East 57th Street in New York, and then in mid-July flew to England, where Marilyn began work on *The Prince and the Showgirl.*

During the next four months while Marilyn was filming, Miller worked with Peter Brook on a revised version of *A View from the Bridge* which opened at the Comedy Theatre in London on 11 October. During the same period he completed a short story based on his experiences in Nevada which he called 'The Misfits'. But also during this period it became evident that Miller could not escape involvement in his new wife's emotional problems. He frequently found himself caught between the actress and irate directors and producers infuriated by her chronic lateness. When he flew back to New York to be with his sick daughter he had to cut short his visit because of his wife's needs. Some time during this period Marilyn read an entry in her husband's notebook in which he expressed some disappointment in her. The incident was traumatic, and may have been the first of what she considered to be a series of betrayals that gradually alienated her trust and affection.

On their return to New York they moved back into their apartment and fixed up a study in which he could write. But the distractions of New York City (and his wife's career) made concentration difficult. In the following summer, therefore, they rented a house on the south shore of Long Island where they spent what was probably the happiest period of their married life. She cooked, did housekeeping, and even fished with her husband; Arthur wrote regularly during the mornings. Furthermore they were expecting their first child, a child that Marilyn desperately wanted. In the autumn this tranquillity was destroyed. One morning Marilyn began complaining of severe cramps, and after an agonising four-hour ride into a Manhattan hospital, she had a miscarriage. In an effort to give her something positive to think about, Miller told Marilyn that he would write a film script for her. When they moved back into Manhattan, however, she was severely depressed and he urged her to go back to work. At his urging, she agreed to appear in the Billy Wilder comedy, *Some Like It Hot*, and shooting for the film began in August 1958. Miller accompanied his wife to Hollywood where once again Marilyn found the work emotionally exhausting. To complicate matters she discovered she was pregnant again. Partly due to her behaviour on the set, filming dragged on until December at which time she had a second miscarriage.

During this period Miller continued to write, but the

demands made on his time and nervous energy by his wife's career were beginning to tell. The play he had been working on in Rhode Island was abandoned, and work on his film, an adaptation of his short story 'The Misfits', proceeded slowly. In the winter of 1959–60 the Millers went to Hollywood where Marilyn was scheduled to film *Let's Make Love* with Yves Montand. Miller left Hollywood for several weeks to consult with John Huston and to examine locations in Nevada. In his absence Marilyn became emotionally involved with Montand.

Filming of *The Misfits* finally started on 18 July 1960. What had begun hopefully, as a gift to Marilyn after her first miscarriage, had somehow turned into a horrible disaster. Although they maintained appearances, they were hardly speaking. They shared the same hotel suite, but travelled to and from the set separately. Once again Marilyn's nerves made her unreliable at work and Miller was forced to sit with her through countless sleepless nights, and to oversee her intake of medication until he himself was on the verge of a nervous breakdown. When the film was finally finished, the couple returned to New York on separate planes and Marilyn announced their plans to begin living apart. In January 1961, she obtained a divorce in Juarez, Mexico.

(ii)

There is little doubt that the failure of his marriage profoundly affected Miller. The relationship in which he had hoped to find a new freedom, openness and spontaneity, had left him instead emotionally drained and tormented by self-doubt. In an effort to pick up the pieces of his life he moved out to his Roxbury farm. There in the peaceful surroundings of the New England countryside he began again the painful process of extracting meaning from experience. About this time he was asked to do a screen adaptation of Albert Camus' novel, *The Fall*. The project fell through, but Miller became fascinated by the ironic picture of moral evasiveness in the French work. He had been working for some time on a play about individuals who had lived through the 1930s and found their ideals in conflict with the course of post-war American life. In his sketches he had been trying to break out of conventional realism by using 'Shakespearean' techniques of juxtaposing characters and incidents.[10] Now the Camus novel suggested a method by which a dramatist might engage his audience more powerfully through the use of direct address. These various experiments were to culminate in *After the Fall*, Miller's first new play to be produced in New York in nine years and in many ways his most experimental and controversial drama.

After the Fall, like much of Miller's work, is the result of interacting public and private circumstances. The external stimulus to complete the play was provided by the establishment of the Repertory Theater of Lincoln Center under the co-direction of Robert Whitehead and Elia Kazan. The company, which was to be patterned on the great repertory companies of Europe, would be a permanent group of actors and theatrical craftsmen dedicated to the theatre as art rather than entertainment. Such at least was the hope of the two directors when they approached Miller in October 1962 and secured his commitment to let them produce his next play.

If it was the prospect of performance by a genuine repertory company that encouraged Miller to be more experimental in his form than he might otherwise have been, it was developments in his personal life that determined the theme of the play. The breakdown of his marriage to Marilyn Monroe was more than a failure in personal relationships; it constituted for Miller a painful confrontation with aspects of his own nature that he had been reluctant to face. The idea that he might have been guilty for the estrangement of his wives was not new; nevertheless, the question acquired a sort of desperate urgency after his meeting with Ingeborg Morath.

Inge Morath had been involved in taking publicity pictures on the set of *The Misfits,* but it was not until she appeared at the Roxbury farm on a new assignment that Miller got to know her. He was attracted by her efficiency and cool-headed courage, and also perhaps by her European background and outlook so different in certain respects from his own. She had been born in Austria in 1924, and had studied in Berlin, Budapest and Vienna. After the war she had married an English journalist, but the marriage had ended in divorce in 1954. Since that time she had taken up photography, and moved to America where she had won a considerable reputation in her new field.

The writing of *After the Fall* occupied Miller until the autumn of 1963 by which time the script ran for five hours. Many of the scenes and incidents undoubtedly go back to work done in the late 50s but it is equally certain that the final version of the play must have been affected by three crucial events in Miller's life during the final two years of its composition: the death of his mother in March 1961, his wedding to Inge Morath in February 1962, and the death of Marilyn Monroe in August 1962.

One other circumstance connected with the production of the play drew attention to its unusually personal nature. This was the reunion after more than a decade of Arthur Miller and Elia Kazan. Kazan had worked closely with the playwright on *All My Sons* and *Death of a Salesman*, and not a little of the success of the first play particularly was due to his brilliant direction. The two men became estranged when Kazan decided to co-operate with the House Committee on Un-American Activities in 1952, and for many years thereafter they did not speak to one another. A reconciliation had been effected partly by Marilyn Monroe and partly by Miller's mellowing attitude brought about by his increased awareness of the complexity of the issues he once thought were so clear. The playwright's concern with these issues is evident in *After the Fall* in a series of scenes dealing with Quentin's relationship to Mickey, a character who seems to be based on Elia Kazan.

Rehearsals began on 24 October and continued for some three months during which Miller continued to shape and rewrite. The play opened in January, not as had been hoped in the Vivian Beaumont Theater in Lincoln Center (still incomplete), but in the ANTA – Washington Square Theatre, a temporary structure hastily erected to house the company.

Reaction to Miller's first play in nine years was mixed. While it proved popular at the box-office and extra performances were scheduled by the company, many critics were outraged by what they considered to be Miller's self-justifying presentation of his relationship with Marilyn Monroe. Although the dramatist stoutly denied that the play was any more autobiographical than his other work, the general perception was that the scenes between Quentin and Maggie were almost embarrassingly documentary. This public display of a private quarrel (as it was generally regarded), questionable enough at any time, seemed to many to be particularly tasteless in view of the relatively recent and widely publicised suicide of the popular actress. Once again, Miller seems to have completely misjudged the effect his play would have on its audience. So preoccupied had he become with the general issues in the drama that he seems to have lost sight altogether of its personal relevance. According to Robert Whitehead, it was not until three months before the play was ready to go into rehearsal that Miller phoned him to state that it had just occurred to him that audiences might mistake Maggie for Marilyn.[11] It is scarcely surprising, therefore, that Miller felt that the reaction to the New York production of the play was distorted, and that the real issues raised by the drama never received the discussion they deserved.

During the summer of 1964, in a period of some five weeks, Miller dramatised a story which he had first heard in 1955. *Incident at Vichy* is set in a police waiting-room during a round-up of suspected Jews in occupied France during the Second World War. It tells of a German aristocrat who is brought to an awareness of his complicity in the Nazi evil and who attempts to atone for his guilt by helping a Jew to escape. It is a rather transparent moral fable on Miller's favourite theme, but skilfully crafted and written with passionate conviction. The play opened on 4 December 1964 to generally favourable reviews.

The following year saw Miller's reputation continue to rise. This was due in part to the revival of two of his earlier plays. In 1965 the National Theatre of Great Britain mounted a production of *The Crucible* under the direction of Sir Laurence Olivier, which was probably the finest performance of the play to that date. Later in the same year, Ulu Grosbard staged a highly successful Off-Broadway revival of *A View from the Bridge*. Also in 1965, Miller was elected International President of PEN (an association of poets, essayists and novelists), in which position he campaigned actively on behalf of writers imprisoned by totalitarian regimes. By the mid-1960s, therefore, it looked as though Miller had come through the apparent 'slump' of a nine-year absence from New York to become once more a powerful force in the American theatre.

The New York successes of 1964–5 were, however, slightly deceptive. Both *After the Fall* and *Incident at Vichy* had been performed as part of a repertory season, and were given only fifty-nine and ninety-nine performances respectively. *A View from the Bridge* achieved a longer run, but it was in the less commercial atmosphere of Off-Broadway. The most ominous sign of the times, however, was the failure of the Repertory Theater of Lincoln Center to realise the ideals of its founders. Some of the actors who had made financial sacrifices to belong to the company began to feel that not everyone involved with the project was equally penalised. The management felt that the budget allocated to the theatre was hopelessly inadequate. Finally, the tension between Robert Whitehead and the Board of Directors erupted when it was discovered that the Board was searching for a new General Manager. Since he had not been informed of the move, Whitehead resigned, and Kazan and Miller left with him, convinced that the Board had no intention of honouring its commitment to support a true repertory system. Whatever hopes Miller might have had of becoming part of a dedicated ensemble of theatre people comparable to the best repertory companies of Europe were shattered. From this point on the playwright would have to find other ways of reaching his public.

(iii)

Some of the difficulties he would encounter were experienced during preparations for the production of *The Price*. The original opening, scheduled for the autumn of 1967, had to be delayed because of casting problems. Rehearsals finally began in December with Ulu Grosbard directing;

however, in the course of rehearsals, Jack Warden, the original Victor, became ill and had to be replaced in the role by Pat Hingle. This delayed the out-of-town première in Philadelphia, and then two days before the New York opening, David Burns had an emergency operation and his understudy had to step into the role of Solomon. To complicate matters further, Miller and Grosbard did not see eye-to-eye on the production, and the playwright took over direction for the last week of Broadway previews. When the play finally opened it was greeted as Miller's most successful work in many years. It ran for 425 performances in New York after which it transferred to London where it ran for another year.

In the decade or so since the success of *The Price*, Miller has seen his American reputation begin to decline while his international stature appears to be on the rise. This paradox is partly a result of the fact that foreign audiences were sometimes slow to see the universal relevance of plays that appeared at first quintessentially American. It is also a consequence of the inflationary conditions on Broadway which make the New York commercial stage more and more hostile to serious drama. The past ten years have seen Miller moving in new directions as a writer. The financial security he has earned from the amateur and foreign performing rights of his plays has made him more independent of Broadway and able to escape its restrictions. Consequently, he has tended to have his plays produced away from Broadway, often by non-commercial managements. Two one-act plays, *Fame* (based on his own short story) and *The Reason Why* (an anti-war allegory about man's instinctive impulses towards violence), were first presented at the New York Theatre Workshop in 1970. *Fame* was subsequently turned into a television drama in 1978, and *The Reason Why* into a short film shot on location in Roxbury. *Up from Paradise,* a musical version of *The Creation of the World*, was given five performances at the Power Center for the Performing Arts at the University of Michigan in April 1974. In 1977 a drama about politics, art and sex in an Iron Curtain country entitled *The Archbishop's Ceiling* was presented for a four-week run at the Eisenhower Theater at the Kennedy Center in Washington. It proved puzzling to the reviewers, and the author has withdrawn it for further revisions. One of the most successful new departures was the television film *Playing for Time*, which Miller adapted from Fania Féne-lon's account of her experience in the women's orchestra at Auschwitz during the Second World War. The two legitimate plays which were brought to Broadway, *The Creation of the World and Other Business* (1972) and *The American Clock* (1980), both fared disastrously.

The Creation of the World is Miller's most radical departure from realism and it was plagued with problems from the beginning. Some of these were related to the choice of Harold Clurman as director. Clurman who had directed *Incident at Vichy* was then near seventy and two generations away from some of the young actors he would be working with. The rehearsal period was marked by misunderstandings, tensions and finally cast-changes. The play opened in October in Boston where Clurman resigned. The Boston reviews were unfavourable, and Miller felt that revisions were necessary. Gerald Freedman was brought in to direct, and in Washington, in consultation with Miller and producer Robert Whitehead, he made further changes in the company. Further previews were scheduled in Boston and New York before the play finally opened on 30 November 1972. Critics who had come to expect a certain kind of social realism from Miller were baffled by his excursion into mythology and the play closed after only twenty performances.

Miller's most recent encounter with the hazards of production on Broadway have simply emphasised once again the hostility of the New York commercial environment to serious work in the theatre. *The American Clock*, which opened on Broadway in November 1980, was originally conceived in the early 1970s when Miller discovered Studs Terkel's oral history of the Depression, *Hard Times*. His first plan was to open the play at the University of Michigan with a student cast, but he became discouraged with the script and set it aside to work on other things. Then in 1974 he saw a staged reading of the work by the Seattle Repertory Company under the direction of Dan Sullivan, and his interest in the script was rekindled. The revival of *The Price* at the Spoleto Festival in Charleston, South Carolina, in 1979, and the successful transfer of that production to Broadway suggested a way to bring this new play into New York. A production of *The American Clock* by the Harold Clurman Theater in New York under the direction of Dan Sullivan opened at the Spoleto Festival in May. The reviews were generally favourable, and extra performances were scheduled in Charleston. When the production was brought to New York in November, however, it fared badly at the box-office and not much better at the hands of the critics. As a result it was withdrawn after only twelve performances.

To a greater extent than most, perhaps, Miller's art has always been a reflection of his life. His personal experiences have shaped his political and philosophical convictions, and his need to understand himself and the life around him is the generating force behind his plays. Miller's work has an organic unity, each play seeming to grow out of earlier ones or to return to familiar themes. Collectively they reveal the efforts of one individual to confront and find some intelligible meaning in the events of the last half-century. If that attempt has led sometimes to disillusionment, it has never led to defeat. In a letter to the Chairman of the House Committee on Un-American Activities in 1956, Miller wrote,

> I was looking for the world that would be perfect. I think it necessary that I do that if I were to develop myself, as a writer . . . . I am not ashamed of this. I accept my life . . . . What I sought to find from without I subsequently learned must be created within.[12]

Miller's drama is a record of that search and of its discoveries.

3
'The Man Who Had All the Luck' and 'All My Sons'

When Arthur Miller began his career in the early 1940s, there were no subsidised theatres, no permanent repertory companies, no avant-garde, not even the alternative commercial theatre that later developed 'Off-Broadway'. Professional theatre was confined almost entirely to New York City, and there it was in the hands of commercial managers. The key figure in the business of presenting plays on Broadway was not the writer nor the director (and certainly not the actor) but the producer. Like a buyer in a large department store, the producer was responsible for putting the merchandise on display. He found the script, hired the director, raised the financial backing, rented the theatre, and generally supervised the budget. His reasons for undertaking these various responsibilities were almost purely monetary. His overriding, if not his only, purpose was to make a profit for himself and a substantial return for his backers.

While it was still possible in the 1940s and 1950s to make a fortune on Broadway, there were signs even then that the system was in trouble. Restrictive union practices and the competition of films and television all contributed to the ills of the theatre industry, but the fatal illness was rapidly rising costs. Between 1939 and 1948, production expenses increased about three-and-one-half times with the result that a play needed to run for several months before the investors could hope to get a return on their money. Because of this pressure, it became unprofitable to continue a production which was only moderately successful. Anything that was not a 'hit' was a 'flop'. By the mid 1960s, about twenty per cent of all shows were closing out of town or in the first week in New York.

Quite apart from the impact the Broadway system had on a play's chances of survival, the 'hit–flop' approach to production affected every aspect of the drama. Actors were hired for a single production and had no opportunity to develop their craft under the continuing supervision of a single artistic director. Consequently they were rarely capable of the kind of ensemble-playing which characterised such permanent companies as the Moscow Art Theatre or the Abbey Theatre in Dublin. Furthermore, plays were usually revised during rehearsals when suggestions from the actors, director and even the producer or backers would be incorporated into the script, sometimes transforming the playwright's intentions altogether. As the risks multiplied, the incentive for producing serious drama declined. Off-Broadway, and then Off-off-Broadway began to provide an alternative to the purely commercial theatre, and to accelerate the flight of the serious audience, leaving the showbusiness field almost entirely to musicals and popular comedy. By 1967, only three per cent of Broadway box-office revenue was earned by serious original American drama.

From time to time groups or individuals have tried to

introduce New Yorkers to a different conception of what theatre can be. Two such organisations active in the 1930s had a profound influence on Miller. The first of these was the Federal Theatre Project for which he wrote briefly after graduation. The most radical challenge to traditional theatre ever to appear in America, the Federal Theatre Project was an attempt to create a genuine people's theatre which would appeal to a working-class audience and reflect broad social concerns in productions spread across the country instead of localised in New York City. Originally conceived as a relief project for theatre workers of all kinds from circus performers to scene painters, it was a branch of the WPA (Works Progress Administration) set up by President Roosevelt in 1935 to combat the massive unemployment created by the Depression. As head of the Federal Theatre Project, the government appointed Hallie Flanagan, a left-leaning and experimental director from Vassar College, who energetically recruited like-minded colleagues from across the country. The project produced revivals of classics as well as new plays, but its most original (and controversial) contribution to the development of the American theatre was the so-called 'living newspaper' productions. These documentary dramas on current social issues were compiled by teams of writers comparable to the staff of a large metropolitan daily. Each production differed, but all employed a wide variety of anti-realistic techniques (from sources ranging from Aristophanes to political cartoons) to make a social comment.

Even more influential on the young Arthur Miller was the Group Theatre active during the decade 1931–41. The Group Theatre, as its name suggests, was a permanent company dedicated primarily to the development of a strong acting ensemble. The actors came to feel that they had something of a social mission. Director Harold Clurman taught them that interest in the life of their times would lead to the discovery of methods by which that life could most truly be presented in the theatre. 'Life was the starting point and an effect on life the aim.'[13] Plays produced by the Group, like other leftist drama of the time, presented life as a social struggle, a dialectic of no and yes, of death and life, disillusionment and faith. The dramatists strove for a synthesis in human concerns and believed that they could affect the destiny of nations. Their vision was one which combined a keen recognition of the spiritual barrenness of contemporary society with an optimistic faith in collectivist philosophy.[14] In the work of such companies, Miller thought he saw the possibility of a drama that could be more than mere entertainment, and which could touch men's minds and consciences as well as their emotions.

In the years following graduation, Miller had little trouble in finding stories for his plays, but considerable difficulty in exploring the meaning of those stories. In this respect, the evolution of *The Man Who Had All the Luck* is characteristic. The central story concerns the fate of an individual who becomes obsessed that his neighbours are plotting against him and who finally commits suicide. In working with this story, however, Miller gradually turned it from a tragedy into something more positive. The published version (issued before the play was revised for production) tells of the rise to prosperity through a series of lucky accidents of the protagonist, David Frieber. By observing those around him, Frieber becomes convinced that his faith in justice is a delusion, and that there is a law of disaster at work in the universe. He feels, however, that he will be safe after he has suffered some set-back, and comes to believe that the disaster in store for him is the death of the child he and his wife are expecting. In preparation for that disaster, and in an effort to measure himself against his fate, David puts most of his property into other people's names, and throws himself into the raising of mink, an enterprise that depends entirely on his own skill and attention. When the expected calamity does not materialise and his baby is born healthy, Frieber becomes even more fearful that some disaster is impending. In the end, when some poisoned feed has been prepared for the animals by mistake, his wife persuades him that he must take fate into his own hands by allowing the mink to die. The act of deliberately ruining himself financially, she argues, will enable him to be at peace, unburdened by money he feels he does not deserve, and content to live on his earnings as a mechanic.

If *The Man Who Had All the Luck* is in some ways a clumsy apprentice piece, it is nevertheless fascinating for what it reveals of Miller's 'archetypal' interests. At one level, the play is an allegory about existential choice. David Frieber is a naive, insecure, self-doubting individual with an acute sense of other people's misfortunes. He begins the play with a jejune optimism that the world is ruled by justice – 'If people don't receive according to what they deserve inside then we're living in a madhouse.'[15] In the course of the action he comes to the equally absurd antithetical conclusion that everyone is punished – 'The world is made that way as if a law was written in the sky somewhere. Nobody escapes! I almost believed I was special in the world, but tonight I know what's waiting for me.' In the end, David is made to realise that the defeatist resignation which holds that man is no more than a helpless jellyfish is wrong. Against the advice to 'lose easily', man must assert the possibility of defiant freedom and take charge of his own fate – 'There was nothing in the sky that gave you things, nothing that could take them away! It was always you.'

The play is significant in another way, too, because in it

Miller discovered a vein of dramatic source-material which was to prove almost inexhaustible. That vein was the father–son relationship represented in *The Man Who Had All the Luck* by Patterson Beeves and his son Amos. In this subplot, Beeves is a disappointed man who has flitted from one job to another without ever finding success and who is consequently determined that his son will not fail as he has done. To this end, he makes him concentrate on one single occupation – pitching – and pins all of his hopes on getting Amos into big-league baseball. When a scout for the Detroit Tigers tells Beeves that his method of training has ruined his son for professional ball, Amos turns on his father in a fury of disappointment, calling him a liar and a fake. The story is a subordinate part of the published play, but in the stage version Miller made Amos and David brothers and found that in writing of the father–son relationship and of the son's search for his relatedness, there was a 'fullness of feeling he had never known before'. In that relationship, 'the crux of *All My Sons* . . . was formed; and the roots of *Death of a Salesman* were sprouted'.[16]

Miller's second Broadway play originated very much as his first had done in a true incident told to him by a friend. This story concerned a family from the Middle West which had been destroyed when the daughter had reported her father to the authorities for selling faulty machinery to the Army. Miller says that he visualised the second-act climax to *All my Sons* almost before the narrator had finished the story. Nevertheless, the actual writing of the work took some two years. In the final version the manufacturer, Joe Keller, has not only shipped out defective airplane parts, but he has also escaped the consequences of his actions by pinning the blame on his partner. Seemingly undisturbed by the death of twenty-one flyers who crashed in planes with his cracked cylinder-heads, Joe Keller has returned to his home, regained the affection of his neighbours, rebuilt his business and generally resumed his successful life. His eldest son, Chris, on his return from war joined the family firm convinced that his father was innocent of the crime for which he was tried and acquitted. Meanwhile, Keller's partner, Steve Deever, who was convicted and is serving a prison sentence has been abandoned by both his children, Ann and George, who have not believed his protestations of innocence. The Deever family has moved from the neighbourhood to avoid the scandal, but Chris has been writing to Ann. Ann had been engaged to the younger Keller son, Larry, who was reported missing in the war and has never been found. The play opens with Ann coming to visit the Kellers on Chris's invitation.

The drama unfolds like a tautly written mystery story. The apparently placid surface of the Keller family life is disturbed first by the arrival of Ann and then by the announcement that George will also be coming to visit. The first act ends with an ominous tension between Joe Keller and his wife, Kate, and with her cryptic warning to him to 'be smart'. The second act reopens the latent conflict between the two families. George has become convinced that his father has been framed by Joe, and he is determined that Ann will not marry Chris. Ann remains sceptical of these new charges, and even George is in danger of being charmed by the Kellers until Kate lets it slip that Joe was not sick, as he had maintained at the trial, on the day the cylinder heads had been delivered. Unable to persuade Ann to go with him, George leaves. In a quarrel with his mother, Chris finally learns the truth, and when he confronts his father, Joe admits that he did give the order to ship out the defective parts.

The third act brings a further revelation in the form of a

letter which Ann had received from Larry just before he had been reported missing. In it he confessed that he had been shattered by the news of his father's arrest and was intending to commit suicide. This news destroys Kate's obsessive belief that Larry is still alive and finally overcomes her opposition to a marriage between Chris and Ann. It also brings home to Joe the full loathsomeness of his antisocial act by making him see that the death of his own son is a direct consequence of his actions. Joe agrees to turn himself in to the district attorney, but instead he goes upstairs and shoots himself.

All My Sons is greatly indebted to the work of Henrik Ibsen, who adapted methods of Greek tragedy to realist drama. Ibsen perfected what has been called 'the play of ripe circumstance' in which, in the course of a relatively short period of stage time, the events of a whole lifetime are put into a perspective which gives tragic significance to the catastrophe. Miller has obviously learned from the Norwegian master how to withhold information about the past until it is most useful dramatically, and how to create a sense of an inexorable web of cause and effect. But *All My Sons* is more than a slavish imitation. The principal difference is in the attitudes of the two dramatists. Whereas Ibsen is primarily concerned with the consequences of past action (the birds coming home to roost), Miller is more interested in the reaction which follows understanding. In Miller, the moment of awareness is always preparation for a moment of choice.

All My Sons can be thought of as operating on three levels of significance: the cosmic, the social and the psychological. Originally, the dramatist gave far more emphasis to Kate's astrological beliefs, but in the course of revision this element of the play was reduced. Kate still goes through a development similar to David Frieber's during which she comes to realise that her faith in astrology is an illusion. Convinced at the opening of the play that 'God does not let a son be killed by his father,' she comes to see that she had been deliberately blinding herself to what she did not want to admit. But Kate's story in the final version of the play is subordinated to those of Joe and Chris, and the major focus appears to be on the conflict between two kinds of social code.

It is this stratum of the play which seems most old-fashioned and didactic. The conflict embodied here is between two sets of values – the one represented by Kate and Joe Keller, the other embodied in different ways in the younger generation of Chris, Ann, George and Larry. The Kellers epitomise the capitalistic system of competition, the 'land of the great big dogs, [where] you don't love a man . . . you eat him'.[17] George and Ann speak for a world of justice, like that of David's hopes, where everyone gets what he deserves. Chris and Larry articulate a still higher ideal, a New Testament law of love and co-operation rather than the Mosaic 'eye for an eye'. For Chris, this ideal is a product of his experience during the war when he saw men who 'killed themselves for each other'. In the destruction and horror of combat, Chris believed, 'one new thing was made. A kind of – responsibility. Man for man', which gave life meaning. Chris's restlessness and moral urgency derive from his sense that that meaning has been lost in civilian life, and that the men who fought and died have been betrayed by those who never understood what the fighting had been about.

The conflict between the generations is complicated, however, by the Kellers' curious incomprehension of the issues. Both Kate and Joe justify what has happened on the ground that is was done with the very best motive – love for their children. Whatever unfortunate consequences Joe's

41

actions may have had on individuals outside the family are rationalised away as inevitable results of the system, or of the 'way the world is'. As Miller says of Joe, he thinks of himself, not as a 'partner in society, but as an incorporated member' who cannot be sued for the wrong doing of the corporation.[18]

The design of *All My Sons*, therefore, is the confrontation of a man with all of the consequences of his actions. It proceeds in two phases. The play is not, like *Oedipus*, the uncovering of an unknown sin so horrible in its author's eyes that he blinds himself; nor is it, like *Hamlet*, the attempt to unmask a criminal anxious to keep his guilt secret. The simple exposing of his unashamed involvement does not bring Keller any new insight into himself or his actions. When Chris confronts him with his deed, Keller continues to excuse himself. In order to bring the play to a conclusion, Joe must see and admit his guilt. This second climax is brought about by Ann. Armed with her letter from Larry, she makes Kate and then Joe give up their delusions about being untouched by the consequences of Joe's actions. Only when tragedy touches him directly does Keller seem able to sympathise with the suffering of others and recognise his connection with the rest of humanity. Even at the end, however, Joe remains evasive. Unable to face trial and imprisonment, he kills himself.

Judging from the title of the play, it is this conflict of social values with which the dramatist is primarily concerned. But there is a deeper, psychological significance in *All My Sons* which is examined less thoroughly. This involves the question of faith, and is closely related to issues raised in *The Man Who Had All the Luck*. Kate's loss of belief has been mentioned, but Miller does not show us in detail how she responds to this disillusionment. In the case of Joe Keller, however, and still more in that of his son, the playwright is interested in exploring the psychological reaction to a loss of faith. Joe Keller has based his life on the conviction that nothing is bigger than the relationship between a father and a son. When he comes to realise that his responsibility is not restricted to his family but extends to a universe of people beyond the property line, he cannot face his own past. His suicide is partly an act of penance for his previous deeds, but it is also the act of a man who cannot live with himself.

Chris, too, is disillusioned in the play when he discovers that his father whom he had idolised is no better than other men. The pain caused by that insight is intense and has the effect of temporarily paralysing his will – 'I never saw you as a man. I saw you as my father. I can't look at you this way. I can't look at myself.' As a result of his sorrow, Chris vacillates between an inability to face his father and an over-zealous vindictiveness. When he hears the shot, he is overcome by doubt and remorse, and it is Kate who encourages him to take control of his life – 'Don't take it on yourself. Forget now. Live.'

4
Death of a Salesman

Death of a Salesman stands apart from almost all of Arthur Miller's other work. Nothing in *The Man Who Had All the Luck* or *All My Sons* prepared New York audiences for the quite extraordinary achievement of *Salesman;* and many critics have never forgiven the playwright for not repeating the triumph. *Salesman* seems both the epitome of everything Miller has aimed for in the theatre and a separate and unique creation. It is the exception to almost every easy generalisation about the dramatist. It was written in almost a single burst of creative inspiration, from personal experience not from an outside source; it contains a deep vein of humour and a compassionate tolerance not always found in Miller's work; it is one of the few instances when the playwright has projected himself into a character quite unlike himself, writing in this play from the point of view of the father rather than the alienated son; and it is Miller's most successful attempt at creating individual characters with universal significance. When he first appeared on the American stage, Willy Loman was recognised as a kind of

American Everyman – a universal symbol made real by hundreds of minutely observed details of speech, manner and psychology.

The most original feature of the play is its form – a form for which Miller had been searching since the beginning of his writing career.[19] *Death of a Salesman* struck New York playgoers as something entirely novel, 'a fresh creation in a style of its own' as Brooks Atkinson described it. The success of the play owes much to the brilliant fusion of various theatrical elements which is a result of the original collaboration of scene-designer, director and playwright. One of the most striking features of the original production was Jo Mielziner's set. Developing ideas he had worked out in *The Glass Menagerie* and *A Streetcar Named Desire,* Mielziner created a skeletal setting which provided three interior playing areas and permitted a variety of other scenes to be played on a large forestage. The house was set against a background which could be transformed by a change of lighting from an oppressive cityscape to a leafy pastoral. This permitted a rapid alternation between the scenes in the present and others from Willy's memory of the past. The production flowed smoothly from the Loman kitchen out into office or restaurant on the forestage, and from fully lit scenes to isolated pools of illumination. The effect was a combination of detailed realism and a more poetic expressionism. The actuality conveyed by accurate period properties such as the 1929 refrigerator was filtered through a haze of affectionate memory which muted the colours, softened the lights and made the characters seem larger than life.

The sense of heightened or poeticised realism in the staging was matched by the acting. Kazan, Lee J. Cobb and Arthur Kennedy had all been with the Group Theatre and the style of the production had its roots in the acting tradition of that company. But the performers were able to transcend the limitations sometimes associated with the rather introverted 'method' style. Lee Cobb particularly, a huge rumpled man with a deep, rich voice, endowed the character of Willy with a dignity beyond his station in life. It was Cobb's ability to lift his performance onto the high plane of tragic acting, to create a character who was exhausted without being weak, misguided rather than insane, that contributed so largely to the impact of the New York production.

The most novel feature of the play, however, was the rich interpenetration of past and present. The great advantage of the Kazan staging was that the present was never erased by the past but was rather made richer by it. Whereas the film version of the play showed Willy's memories as flashbacks – substituting one time and place for another – the stage production shows past and present existing simultaneously. The result is an enlargement of the scope of the dramatic form to include the world of subjective experience normally excluded from the stage. It is the very richness of *Death of a Salesman* which is at once its greatest strength and its principal problem. On the one hand, the form permits an intricate interweaving of thematic material in which incidents are thrust into the play with a minimum of exposition and developed only so long as they are thematically relevant.[20] On the other hand, the mixture of verbal and theatrical images defies simple analysis and conveys to many readers and spectators an impression of narrative confusion. This is largely due to the fact that the story proceeds in two dimensions – real time and remembered time. The 'external plot' deals with the last twenty-four hours of Willy's life from his return home late Sunday night to his death Monday evening. Then there is the 'internal plot' which treats the past from Willy's earliest memories of his own father to the fateful summer of Biff's failure in high school. In outline, the play is very similar to an Ibsenite play of ripe circumstance except that the exposition of events from the past is dramatised instead of being simply reported. This similarity makes it possible to discuss the work as a play of social criticism not unlike *All My Sons* in which one might look for the central conflict in the opposed value-systems of the two main characters. According to such a view, *Salesman* is an indictment of the American capitalist system which values machines more highly than men. The central scene takes place in Howard's office where Willy's pleading for his job and invoking his human connection with Howard is cruelly juxtaposed with Howard's indifferent insistence that 'business is business' and with the mechanical imitation of human voices on the wire recorder. The difficulty with this interpretation is that it simplifies the play, ignoring the humane capitalist, Charley, and forgetting altogether that Willy is a very active collaborator in his own downfall.

Another related approach to the play is to see it as a domestic social drama in which the central character is Biff. This interpretation would identify the central conflict as being between Willy's determination to make Biff into a success in capitalistic terms, and his son's search for a more valid life as a man who works with his hands. Here the playwright's earlier examinations of father–son conflicts in *Luck* and *Sons* seem to anticipate the opposition between Willy's phoney doctrine of materialistic success and Biff's perception of a more humane ideal based on the freedom and companionship of the American west. But once again such an interpretation seems a distortion of the play. While it is true that Biff represents the possibility of undeluded integrity, it is not clear precisely what kind of social order he embodies, not is it at all apparent that we are to prefer Biff's rather unimaginative bumbling to his father's irrepressible hopefulness. Finally, the experience of the play makes it impossible for spectators or readers to respond to Biff as the central character because of the overwhelming presence of Willy.

It is the presentation of Willy's internal life which is the most striking feature of the play and the one which must be understood before a final assessment of the work can be made. Willy's memories do not materialise at random. They are triggered by certain incidents in the present, and Willy is changed by remembering them. A detailed examination of this process is impossible, but a single example may illustrate the point. Willy's first return to the past in the play is the result of his recollection of the time when Biff seemed so full of promise. It is brought on by Biff's return home and the inevitable tension between the two men which is a consequence of Biff's apparent inability to settle down. It begins with Willy remembering his son waxing the car and proceeds to recollections of other details such as the way in which Biff 'borrowed' a football from the school locker-room. The guilt Willy felt even then about exaggerating his own accomplishments and encouraging his sons to disregard the law is suggested by the appearance of Linda in the memory.

Since Willy could never deceive his wife with quite the same facility that he could impress his sons, Linda serves as a kind of conscience making him confess his true earnings and his real sense of inadequacy – 'The trouble is, Linda, people don't seem to take to me.'[21] The temporary feeling of intimacy with his wife reminds Willy that he has not even been honest with Linda, and he attempts to justify his infidelity to himself – 'I get so lonely – specially when business is bad . . . . I get the feeling that I'll never sell anything again, that I won't make a living for you, or . . . a business for the boys.' But even this rationalisation is undercut by the intrusion of the image of the woman in the Boston hotel room and the reminder that, in some ways, he had been more generous to his mistress than to his wife. As he approaches the final unspeakable fear – the possibility that he has betrayed Biff too by the double folly of lying and being found out – the voices become more and more accusing. Nevertheless Willy represses the memories and cries out his denial – 'I never in my life told him anything but decent things.' When he returns to the present he is like a man who has glimpsed the ultimate horror, and his immediate impulse is to protect his innocence. At first he tries to blame his failure on tactics or an error in strategy – 'Why didn't I go to Alaska with my brother Ben . . . . What a mistake!' But the memories pushing up into his consciousness will not let him accept that lie. The first recollection of Ben shows Willy's subconscious fear that the things he has been telling his sons were not always as decent as he had claimed – 'I've been waiting for you so long! What's the answer?'

This subtle exploration of Willy's subjective life has led many critics to approach the play as a psychological drama with strong Freudian colouring. According to this interpretation, the work concentrates on family relationships and especially on the conflicts between fathers and sons. This is a more fruitful path into the complexities of the work than the two previously discussed, for father–son conflicts are all-pervasive. Indeed one of the most striking characteristics of Willy is that he is both father and son. The quintessential boy–man, Willy is the eternal adolescent arrested at an early stage of development and because of it unable to help his own son to a healthy maturity. In a very real sense Willy and Biff are more like brothers than father and son, and it is Biff who grows up first.

Willy's problems as a father are shown to be a direct result of his own deprivation as a son, and it is part of the richness of *Death of a Salesman* that its perspective encompasses three generations. Willy's memories touch on the critical moments of his life and the earliest of these concern his hazy recollections of his own father – 'All I remember is a man with a big beard, and I was in Mama's lap, sitting around a fire, and some kind of high music.' The music, of course, is the flute music which sounds periodically through the play and which, Miller informs us in the stage directions, tells of 'grass, trees and the horizon'. The pastoral associations of the music are related to the wanderings of the Loman family 'through Ohio, and Indiana, Michigan, Illinois, and all the Western states' where the elder Loman made and sold his flutes. But the father-image evoked by the music is much more complex than is sometimes suggested. For, according to Ben at least, their father was also a 'great inventor' who 'with one gadget' could make more in a week than Willy would make in a lifetime. The patriarch of the Loman family is therefore a shadowy ideal who embodies a variety of qualities. Musician, craftsman, salesman, inventor (as well as wife-deserter), he is a combination Wandering Jew and Yankee pedlar who has left a mingled heritage to his sons.

Since their father left when Willy was a child, he remains a dim figure in his son's imagination. Willy's determination to give strong guidance to his sons is a result of his sense of the lack of such guidance in his own life. 'Dad left when I was such a baby . . . I never had a chance to talk to him and I still feel – kind of temporary about myself.' Willy has chosen to imitate the salesman side of his father, not through any urging on his father's part but rather as a result of circumstances. The most influential of these was his meeting with David Singleman, an old New England salesman who came to represent for Willy the father he never knew. It is Singleman's life, and more especially his death, that come to symbolise what Willy thinks he wants for himself. As he explains to Howard,

> Old Dave, he'd go up to his room, y'understand, put on his green velvet slippers – I'll never forget – and pick up his phone and call the buyers, and without even leaving his room, at the age of eighty-four, he made his living. And when I saw that, I realised that selling was the greatest career a man could want.

Miller almost certainly intended the irony implied by Willy's interest in a job that required no more effort than lifting a phone, but the more dreadful irony relates to the interpretation of business which Willy derives from Singleman's example. What Singleman's achievement represents to Willy is a demonstration of the co-operative and benevolent nature of capitalism. Singleman's ability to sell by phone at age eighty-four was proof to Willy that he was 'remembered and loved and helped by so many different people'. This conclusion seemed to be confirmed by Singleman's funeral which was attended by hundreds of salesmen and buyers. Singleman, in other words, represented free enterprise with a human face, and it is part of Willy's tragedy that he never realises that such a system does not exist.

Willy's inability to see the nature of the system in which he functions is the more extraordinary in that part of him worships the very ruthlessness that helps to destroy him. The other side of his father – the inventive and irresponsible side – is epitomised in the play by Ben who, as Willy's older brother, constitutes another substitute father-figure. The character of Ben differs from all the other figures in the play in several respects. There is a quality of unreality about Ben which suggests the generalised characters of Expressionist drama. He refuses to answer questions about himself and communicates cryptically – 'when I walked into the jungle, I was seventeen. When I walked out I was twenty-one. And, by God, I was rich!' There is no attempt on Miller's part to reveal Ben's psychological make-up, and indeed the character seems almost a two-dimensional projection of Willy's imagination. Ben is the only character who appears to Willy out of an historical context, and he seems at times to be more like a ghost or *alter ego*. It is probable that he represents in part Willy's depression over his brother's recent death and the breaking of the last connection with his father. But perhaps he functions primarily as a dramatic embodiment of those qualities of assurance, daring and lack of scruples which Willy secretly admires but does not possess. The 'jungle' where no one fights fair is where Willy knows the wealth is to be found, but his own nature yearns for the security of home, garden and an adoring family.

One aspect of the play, therefore, deals with Willy Loman as a son trying to please a father he never knew. His own nature is ill-suited for the competitive world of business and he tries to adjust in two ways. He convinces himself and his sons that success is a product of being well-liked, but at the same time he encourages competitive and even unlawful behaviour. He fails because he never understands the inconsistency in his beliefs and that his desire for the emotional security of popularity is at odds with the realities of the profession he has entered.

CHARLEY: The only thing you got in this world is what you can sell. And the funny thing is that you're a salesman, and you don't know that.

WILLY: I've always tried to think otherwise, I guess.

Willy's failure to come to terms with his own father cripples him in his ability to be a father in his turn. Deprived of affection as a child, he smothers his own sons with love, and oppresses them with the nakedness of his hopes for their success. Here it is important to comprehend the paradoxical nature of the 'conflict' between Willy and his children. For what Hap, and especially Biff, have to fight is not indifference or hostility, but a surfeit of love. The terrible irony of the play is that Willy's struggles, sacrifice and final suicide are not for his own material advancement, but for his sons. Even when Biff is thirty-four years old Willy cannot rid himself of the compulsion to help him. When Charley gives him the advice of the practical realist Willy cannot take it.

CHARLEY: He won't starve. None a them starve. Forget about him.

WILLY: Then what have I got to remember?

CHARLEY: You take it too hard. To hell with it. When a deposit bottle is broken you don't get your nickel back.

It is this overwhelming need to have his sons succeed that is the underlying drive of his life and the cause of his tragic agony.

From the point of view of his sons, therefore, when they understand this love, Willy is a 'prince'. But Biff has had an opportunity to get to know Willy better than Willy ever knew his father, and he has come to realise that Willy is also a 'phoney'. It is the ambivalence of Biff's attitude to his father, and the defensiveness it arouses in Willy, that together cause the conflict between them. The form of the play, however, precludes a full examination of that conflict. Since only Willy's memories are dramatised, the opposition is seen almost entirely from Willy's point of view. It is his shock and guilt we feel when Biff discovers him in the Boston hotel room, not Biff's. And although we understand that Biff then loses faith in his father's ability to influence his teacher, and that he suddenly sees the discrepancy between what Willy pretends to be and what he really is, we never learn exactly how that shock affects his subsequent life.

True, we are told about the externals – that he burned his University of Virginia sneakers, refused to go to summer school to upgrade his math mark, and then embarked on a seventeen-year programme of failure – but we never grasp the precise connection between Biff's disillusionment with his father and his own inability to know himself. For when the play begins, Biff is still torn between resentment of his father and emotional dependence on him. He feels 'like a boy', unable to compromise with the world, but uncomfortable at home. His rejection of his father as a 'fake' at fifteen has in no way altered his need to please him. It is only in the course of his last visit home that he at last seems to understand the emotional block which has been crippling him. After stealing the pen from Bill Oliver's desk he is finally prompted to ask the all-important question: 'Why am I trying to become what I don't want to be?' At that moment he realises that 'all I want is out there, waiting for me the minute I say I know who I am!'

There is on the face of it no obvious reason why Biff did not make this discovery years ago (or conversely, what it was that triggered it at this particular moment). One of the problems Miller himself came to see in the play was that Biff's achievement of self-understanding is not fully enough documented and is overshadowed by Willy's delusion and defeat. It is hard to agree with this criticism altogether because it seems evident that the play Miller has written is not, after all, fundamentally about father–son relationships, nor is the documenting of Biff's disillusionment central to Miller's concerns. Those, it seems to me, are ultimately more philosophical than psychological.

The most fruitful approach to the play, therefore, is to see it like *Luck* and *Sons* as a drama about self-delusion. Miller's central preoccupation is not social, not psychological, but existential. Throughout his career the playwright has been preoccupied with the role the individual plays in his own fate. Why do people behave so differently in moments of crisis? Why, for example, were some men crushed by the Depression while others survived unscathed? Since the external factors were more or less the same for everyone in the 1930s, clearly the differences were within. Those who believed in the system felt guilty for their failure and gave up the struggle. The secret of survival seemed to lie in the discovery of the hidden laws. In the pursuit of this discovery the greatest obstacle was not the absence of facts, but the wilful blindness that rendered many people incapable of seeing those facts. At its core, *Death of a Salesman* is a play about the destructive nature of dreams.

The distinction between psychological and philosophical in this context is a fine one and perhaps involves no more than a difference of emphasis. For clearly the question of belief is both intellectual and emotional. It is Miller's insistence on this fact that underlies the peculiar blend of sex and politics in his plays. The mixture has confused some critics and annoyed others who do not see the connection between the subjects. In *Salesman,* for example, the scene in the Boston hotel room has seemed to some an unnecessary embellishment unrelated to the main theme of the play. Such critics would argue that Biff's discovery of his father's infidelity is not closely connected with his rejection of Willy's doctrine of being well-liked. Miller's point, however, seems to be that it was in fact the shock of Biff's discovery that prevented him from seeing the truth about himself for so long. His anger with his father serves as an excuse to avoid looking for the real causes of his failure which are in himself.

Looked at as a play about knowing, *Salesman* focuses on the conflict between facts as they are, and the attempts of various persons to ignore or disguise those facts. The conflict is not embodied in any particular moment of crisis (except perhaps in the last scene between Willy and Biff), but it is all-pervasive. The Lomans engage in constant deception to conceal the truth from themselves. In different ways Charley, Barnard, Howard and Ben each present Willy with facts that he will not recognise as such. Biff's gradual recognition of what has gone on in the house and his determination to tell Willy the truth appear to the others as a betrayal. In the final confrontation between the two men, Biff cannot make his father face the truth. Willy has too much emotional capital tied up in his dreams of Biff's magnificence, and he prefers to sacrifice his life rather than his illusion. The ending is ironic in that Miller intends the audience to see that Willy is deluded and that a way out exists. As Willy says of Biff, the door of his life was wide open if he had had the courage to go through it. The 'tragedy' of Willy Loman's suffering and death is that they are unnecessary.

Miller has often said that he was surprised by the reaction to *Salesman* because he had thought the play much more hopeful than audiences found it to be. One wonders, however, if such remarks are not a trifle ingenuous. For the epilogue Miller has written for the play (called a requiem in the text) seems something of a dramatic *non sequitur*. To begin with it is an almost shameless exploitation of pathos. The scene of Linda at the graveside, her powerfully moving final speech with its achingly ironic concluding cry 'We're free . . . we're free', and particularly the background flute music, are devices aimed unerringly at the tear ducts. The impression that Willy is a pathetic victim is reinforced by Charley who (somewhat inconsistently) provides in the epilogue the play's most eloquent justification for Willy's romantic hopefulness.

> A salesman . . . don't put a bolt to a nut, he don't tell you the law or give you medicine. He's a man way out there in the blue, riding on a smile and a shoeshine. And when they start not smiling back – that's an earthquake. . . . Nobody dast blame this man. A salesman is got to dream, boy. It comes with the territory.

It seems clear from the rest of the play, however, that we are intended to blame Willy (as Biff certainly does) for having all the wrong dreams. Or perhaps it would be more accurate to say that we are to blame him for holding on to those dreams long after they cease to correspond with any possible reality.

Perhaps the apparent inconsistency is a result of Miller's own ambivalent feeling towards his characters. Certainly there is no question that the world of Willy Loman is the world of Arthur Miller's youth. Not only was Willy patterned on a salesman who worked for Miller's father, but there are numerous parallels between the events in the play and Miller's own life. Like Biff, Miller was a poor student and a good athlete who failed to get into university and worked at a variety of odd jobs before finding his true vocation. When he did decide to become a writer, he had to wait almost seventeen years (from 1932 until *All My Sons* in 1947) before he could justify his career in terms that his father could understand. More important than the personal correspondences, however, are the patterns of emotional and ideological conflicts in the play. As one critic has pointed out, the drama is not about an unsuccessful salesman so much as it is about a Jewish family.[22] The tight family bond, the intense pressure on the eldest son, the strong rivalry between close friends, the anxiety to fit in and be popular are all a little more understandable in a Jewish immigrant context. Furthermore, the speech patterns of the play seemed to this critic to be more natural in Yiddish translation than in the original. Finally, the tone of the work – a blend of pathos and irony – is very close to Jewish literature with its long tradition of turning pain into humour. One strong effect of *Salesman* (as of some other of Miller's plays) is of a secret personal drama partially concealed beneath the seemingly innocent text.

Critical reaction to *Death of a Salesman* has been sharply and often heatedly divided. Sometimes the differences between critics have been along 'ideological' lines – socialists seeing the play as an indictment of capitalism, and salesmen viewing it as a celebration of their profession. Not infrequently they can be attributed to different critical assumptions. The more relentlessly intellectual American critics, led perhaps by Eric Bentley, have tended to decry Miller's lack of intellectual rigour. Such critics tend to attack what they take to be the author's personal beliefs rather than confining themselves to a discussion of the self-contained world of the drama. Ultimately, however, the differences seem to come down to a question of temperament. Plays like *Death of a Salesman* seem to separate critics into what William James would have called the 'tough-minded' and the 'tender-minded' camps. The 'realistic', 'scientific', 'objective' personality often finds Miller sentimental or naive. Willy Loman to such critics is a weak, deluded, child–man – a figure of pathos not tragedy. The world of the play, just because it is the world of the common man is inherently uninteresting because it excludes the extremes of divine idiot and creative genius. Tender-minded critics on the other hand, acknowledge the limitations of Willy's character and world, but see them as strengths not weaknesses. Speaking not for all such critics but only for myself, I respond more strongly to Willy's universality than I do to many more exceptional tragic heroes. As for Willy's blindness, that too seems to me a more valid representation of man's contemporary experience than the 'enlightenment' provided by some acknowledged tragedies. Furthermore, it is ultimately the audience's enlightenment which is important, not the character's, and in this respect I do not think *Death of a Salesman* fails. What emerges at the end of the play seems to me an appropriate blend of pity, fear and consolation – pity for Willy, fear that we may be as self-deluding as he, and hope based on the knowledge that we can, if we so decide, take control of our lives. I doubt if we can ask more of serious drama in the twentieth century.

5
The Crucible

As the title suggests, the central action of *The Crucible* is comparable to the purification of a substance by heat. John Proctor undergoes a metaphorical calcination in the course of which he is reduced to his essential, purified self. The movement of the play is reductive, stripping the central character of layers of protective covering until in the end he stands naked – totally exposed. It is a dramatic pattern very different from the conventional design of Greek or Christian tragedy. In these latter, the hero's suffering is seen to bear a direct relationship to some 'flaw' or error of judgement for which he must accept some responsibility. Usually, too, this suffering leads to some kind of insight into the inevitable relationship between character and fate, and to an acceptance on the part of the protagonist and the audience of the ultimate justice of fate. Miller's play, while it subjects the central character to suffering as great as any tragedy, does so to different effect. Proctor's story is not one of defeat and acceptance, but of triumph and vindication. Whereas the conventional tragic hero is a deluded or obsessed individual in an ordered universe, Proctor is a just man in a universe gone mad.

It is useful to make these distinctions at the outset since *The Crucible* is in many ways the most confusing and misunderstood of Miller's works. The play was coolly received on Broadway when it was first produced, partly because the kind of theatrical magic that contributed so much to the success of *Salesman* was missing. It is a paradox that while *The Crucible* deals with a period remote from the average American's experience, it nevertheless seems a much more earthbound play than *Death of a Salesman*, which presents material that is almost tiresomely familiar. This at least was the effect of the solidly realistic settings of Boris Aronson. The attention paid to the gaunt and pitiless details of the Salem environment was paralleled by the concentration on externals in the direction. Jed Harris, the director of the first New York production, lacked Kazan's flair for drawing hidden resources from his actors and several critics felt that the performances lacked depth and complexity. Harris focused on externals – the scenes of public confrontation between Proctor and Danforth, or Proctor and Abigail. His emphasis was on suspense, action and excitement, on what *New York Times* critic, Brooks Atkinson, called 'nerves' rather than 'heart.' The effect was to underline the melodramatic features of the work and to suggest a clear distinction between the innocent and the guilty characters in the play.

A rare opportunity to revise the work presented itself in the early summer when it became necessary to mount a simpler, less expensive production to go on tour. Miller wrote an extra scene between Proctor and Abigail which was inserted into the play. He also redirected the production himself, setting it against a plain background of black drapes which threw more focus on the character relationships and less on the oppressive surroundings. He created a much more fluid production with minimal properties and lighting, and seemed able to draw more warmth and variety from the actors. In the leading roles, E.G. Marshall and Maureen Stapleton projected a more rustic sincerity than had Arthur Kennedy and Beatrice Straight in the original cast. This second version gave more weight to the intimate scenes between John and Elizabeth in which it is evident that Proctor is far less innocent, far more self-critical than he appears in his public stances.

Although Miller had long been fascinated with the Salem story there can be little doubt that the immediate inspiration for the play was his perception of the effects of the atmosphere of terror inspired by the investigation of the communist 'conspiracy' in America in the late 1940s and 50s. What came to interest Miller about the phenomenon of public terror, however, was not the workings of fear, but the much more bizarre and intricate mechanism of guilt. He became convinced that the root cause, both of the ferocity of the persecution and of the willing, almost eager, surrender of conscience on the part of the accused, was a deeply implanted sense of blame which in the case of the accused could only find release through confession. This handing over of conscience by individuals to the state seemed to Miller the central and informing fact of the 1950s. But the difficulty of exploring such subjects as guilt, confession, atonement and conscience in the modern context is that modern man's understanding of these phenomena is limited. Miller saw in the New England Puritans a group with the kind of moral self-awareness which would enable him to deal with the subject in a manner that would remain, in its essentials at least, realistic.

The Salem witch-trials represent one of the blackest

pages of American history, a horrible aberration of that Puritan spirit of independence which has contributed much to the finest parts of the American national character. In a wave of hysteria that swept the town of Salem in 1692, nineteen adults and two dogs were hanged for witchcraft, and one man was pressed to death for refusing to plead. The evidence of supernatural influence brought against the accused consisted originally of the testimony of a number of girls and young women ranging in age from nine to twenty. This testimony was supported by a number of physical symptoms such as fainting, or hysterical fits. Since those accused of witchcraft could save their lives by confessing and identifying other witches, it is not surprising that suspicion spread rapidly. The witch-hunt ended when a group of church leaders in Boston declared that the unsupported evidence of witnesses was insufficient to justify the death penalty. Before the court had been discredited, however, more than 150 persons had been accused and confined to prison to await trial.

The Salem witch-hunt shares similarities with many other persecutions in history, but in certain respects it is a peculiar product of its time. The Puritan theocracy of New England imposed numerous restraints on its citizens which contributed to an atmosphere of anxiety and repression. These psychological pressures were compounded by the very real danger from Indian raids and from the loss by the colony of certain religious privileges granted under the original charter. Furthermore, the colonists were ill-prepared to understand aberrant behaviour or to deal with the hysteria that followed the suspicion of witchcraft. In their exclusive reliance on religion as the foundation of science and law as well as ethics, the Puritan ministers were confounded by the fact that although the Bible stated explicitly that witches should not be allowed to live, nowhere did it define witchcraft or explain how its practitioners should be identified. The belief then current in Europe as well as America was that witchcraft was a contract or 'covenant' between an individual and the Devil to work for the overthrow of the Christian community. Witches were believed to communicate with the Devil in the shape of small animals or birds known as familiars, to be able to cause mischief to those they disliked by sending out their 'spirit', and to attempt to recruit others to their evil work by appearing to them in dreams or visions. The Salem judges, therefore, relied on three kinds of evidence: unusual marks on the witch's body that might be evidence of a 'witch's teat'; mischief following quarrels between neighbours; and, most especially, accounts of the activities of the witch's 'spectral shape'. Since this latter so-called spectral evidence was by its nature invisible to all but the victim or those gifted with 'second sight', the bulk of the testimony in the Salem trials is of a kind that is completely unverifiable.

There were several aspects of the Salem witch-craze that might well have baffled the most conscientious investigator. To begin with, the chief witnesses were perceived to be in genuine torment. Few of those who reported their actions could doubt that the symptoms of fainting, convulsions, bloody wounds and so on, were accompanied by real pain. Since it was inconceivable to them that apparently innocent children, some of them barely into their teens, would voluntarily inflict such pain on themselves, the inevitable deduction was that they were being afflicted. A second circumstance that seemed to most observers to corroborate the stories of the children was the fact that approximately one quarter of those accused of witchcraft confessed to the crime and gave substantiating details. Finally, once the presence of agents of the 'invisible world' had been established, nothing could any longer be taken at face value. Since Satan himself had appeared glorious before he fell, no evidence of virtuous life was a guarantee that an individual had not been seduced by the Devil and was serving him while pretending outward piety. In such an atmosphere of twisted logic, hardly anyone once named could escape conviction.

Nevertheless, when every allowance is made for the complexity of the situation, it is a fact that the witch-hunt did not affect the whole of New England, but was confined to Salem and a few neighbouring villages. There were particular forces at work in Salem which set it apart and released passions that were elsewhere kept under control. It is this aspect of the case, perhaps, which contributes most ·to the peculiar fascination which the event has exercised over historians ever since. What was it that made the villagers of Salem so particularly susceptible to a madness, which, although by no means confined to Puritan New England, is nevertheless not a universal characteristic of human society? Marion Starkey in *The Devil in Mas-sachusetts* attributes the hysteria to several causes: the unsettled political situation, the neuroticism of the adolescent girls, the presence in the village of the exotic slave, Tituba, and the particularly bitter rivalries and animosities between families and factions. In her account she focuses on the psychology of the children in whose adolescent emotionalism she sees the main cause of the tragedy.[23]

Miller's interest in the story is very different. He sees the accusations of the girls as little more than a catalyst for the reaction whose true causes are in the community. For Miller, Salem represents a microcosm of human society as a whole. His interest was less in the accusers than in the defendants, and especially those who confessed to their 'sins'. What conceivable feelings could lead an individual to admit to a crime that he did not commit? The answer, Miller seems to conclude, is 'terror and guilt'.

The nature of that guilt, which suddenly made the dramatic structure of the play clear to Miller, was suggested by the discovery that Mary Warren tried to exclude John Proctor from accusations of witchcraft while she was denouncing his wife. This hint of a sexual interest in the girls gave Miller a form of motivation that would be more understandable and theatrically effective than amorphous adolescent hysteria. Unfortunately, Mary Warren's role among the accusers was much smaller than that of Abigail Williams whose youth (she was twelve at the time) made unlikely the kind of sexual involvement that twenty-year-old Mary Warren might have had with Proctor. Accordingly, the dramatist altered Abigail's age to seventeen and transformed her into a kind of pagan bacchante. By focusing primarily on the relationship of Abigail, Proctor and Elizabeth, Miller was able to explore two subjects of interest to him – the nature and effect of guilt, and the right of society to judge the actions of its members.

The drama begins very shortly after the precipitating crisis. Ruth Putnam and Betty Parris are in a state of semi-consciousness following their participation in a seance and dance in the woods near the village. In the course of Reverend Parris's questioning it transpires that the evening involved superstitious and pagan rituals which point to a dark subterranean level beneath the apparently pious social order of Salem. Mercy Lewis's dancing and Mary Warren's watching indicate little more than frustration and curiosity, but the actions of two of the girls go far beyond adolescent hijinks. Ruth Putnam had been sent by her mother to commune with the dead, and Abigail Williams had tried to ensure the death of the wife of her lover, John Proctor. The bizarre encounter in the woods would probably have ended without incident if it had not been discovered by Reverend Parris, who so frightened the girls that the youngest of them succumbed to some form of hysterical reaction. The play opens with the adults of Salem trying to ascertain the cause of the children's fits.

The opening act, which Miller calls an overture, introduces us to the principal characters in the play and establishes the pattern according to which Miller believes events unfold. The characters can be arranged rather crudely into three groups. First there are the representatives of the establishment, Parris and the wealthy Putnams. Next come the ordinary citizens of the village, the Nurses, the Coreys and Proctor. Finally there is the outsider, Hale, a representative of the higher authority of learning. It is soon evident that the village is split into factions based in part on wealth and in part on different attitudes to social obligations. On one side are Parris and the Putnams, both what we would call neurotic, both concerned with the maintenance of authority and both, in different ways, eager to blame others for their own limitations or shortcomings. At the other extreme is Rebecca Nurse, well-to-do, but as a result of earned, not inherited, wealth, naturally maternal, and aware that the community members should blame themselves rather than look outside for causes for their troubles.

Between these two factions stand John Proctor and Giles Corey. The latter is cantankerous and ready to blame the Devil for his litigious nature, but it is clear that Miller intends us to sympathise with this likeable crank. It is John Proctor, however, who is the central figure in the play, and his deeply divided nature is reflected in his relationships with his neighbours. The most fatal and mysterious of these relationships is his liaison with Abigail. Miller tells us that Proctor feels he has sinned against his own vision of decent conduct, but the farmer betrays no sign of such feeling in the opening scene. He appears unembarrassed by Abigail's presence and even smiles knowingly at her when he accuses her of being 'wicked'. He says that their relationship is over (even going so far as to say they 'never touched'), but he admits that he may have been drawn to her since she left his house. It seems clear that we are to attribute at least a little of Abby's 'wildness' and sensuality to her relationship with John, and to assume that the 'knowledge' which Proctor put in Abigail's heart is not simply carnal, but also includes some awareness of the hypocrisy of some of the Christian women and convenanted men of the community. This 'radical' side of Proctor's nature is further illustrated by his resentment of Parris's arbitrary use of his authority in calling in Hale without consulting the wardens, and by his opposition to the preacher's enforcement of discipline by hell-fire preaching. Proctor's is not a simple personality like that of Rebecca Nurse, but we are given only hints of his complexity in the first act.

In addition to introducing the characters, the first scene also illustrates Miller's analysis of the hysteria that affects Salem. The exact nature of the malady suffered by Ruth Putnam and Betty Parris is not made clear. Betty presumably fainted in fright when she was discovered by her father, but since Ruth was at the seance at the behest of her mother, there seems to be no reason for her to exhibit the same guilty reaction. Miller is less interested in the ultimate cause of the girls' fits, however, than in the response those fits provoke among the townspeople. That response he shows to be standard and constantly repeated. It begins with the victim of some misfortune or hostility attempting to place the blame outside himself. Ann Putnam blames witchcraft for the death of her children, Parris blames the Devil for his own unpopularity, Abigail blames Tituba for persuading her to drink the blood which she took as a charm against Elizabeth Proctor's life, and finally Tituba blames the Devil for her participation in the ritual. The last is most instructive since it shows so clearly how Tituba is first terrified by threats of whipping and hanging, and then coached in her responses. Her 'confession' is further elicited by promises of forgiveness and security so that the victim of the interrogation is offered release from fear and a considerable emotional reward for her co-operation. Part of Miller's point here is that this process goes on unconsciously so that neither the victim nor the interrogator is fully aware of the projection of guilt.

The second act takes place eight days after the arrival of Hale, and we learn that the Salem court has that afternoon passed its first death sentence. We also learn that Proctor had told Elizabeth that he would give evidence that would discredit the children as witnesses, but that he has delayed going to the court. Subsequent developments that afternoon indicate that that delay was fatal. It seems fairly clear that Miller intends the audience to view Proctor ironically. His lying to Elizabeth about his interview with Abigail, his reluctance to expose her, his rather hypocritical efforts to please his wife by praising the stew to which he has added extra salt, his lashing out at her in response to her criticism, all of these are the actions of a man who is rationalising in order to avoid facing himself. Like many troubled individuals, Proctor is happier with external conflict than he is with inner strife. Proctor's opposition to Parris, his browbeating of Mary Warren, his threatening violence against the court clerk, and his tearing of the Governor's warrant, all suggest a man of strong convictions. But they are more likely in this case the acts of a man who fears moral complexities and for that reason likes to reduce issues to black and white. Far from presenting Proctor as the one just man in a community of cowards, Miller is suggesting that at this point in the play Proctor is as guilty as any of projecting his own faults onto others. When Hale admonishes him by saying 'the world goes mad, and it profit nothing you should lay the cause to the vengeance of a little girl,'[24] Proctor accuses the minister of cowardice. But it is the cry of a man who knows his own paralysing fear. Hale continues, 'Let you counsel among yourselves; think on your village and what may have drawn from heaven such thundering wrath upon you all.' As Proctor knows, Hale might very well be speaking of his liaison with Abby, and he finally resolves to try to bring out the truth. But even at this point he attempts to avoid implicating himself. He threatens Mary Warren to force her to confess to the court that the evidence against his wife is fraudulent, but when Mary tells him that Abigail will charge him with lechery, he hesitates 'with deep hatred of himself'. He finally realises, however, that he can no longer hide his true nature. The hypocrisy and pretence must be ripped away and he must appear naked to the world. The horror this thought inspires in Proctor is the key to his character. For it seems less the deed than the exposure of the deed that troubles him. In fairness, however, we should add that fear of nakedness only occurs in those who are deeply ashamed.

The third act dealing with Proctor's vain attempts to overthrow the court contains one of the most powerful scenes in Miller's work. Here the focus is once again on the public domain and on the officials and institutions of society. Proctor's inner drama is subordinated temporarily to the question of the general hysteria, and once again Miller traces the way in which self-interest corrupts the process of justice. Each of the officials upholding the court – Danforth, Hathorn and Parris – has a personal stake in its continuation. Only Hale seems capable of sufficient objectivity to judge the merit of the evidence submitted by the defence. And, as in the earlier scene, blunders and irrationality are the result of threatened self-interest. Danforth seems ready to listen to the critical witnesses until he is convinced that Proctor wishes to destroy the court and damage the Deputy Governor's reputation. From that point on, his prejudices blind him. Not only is he reluctant to let a lawyer argue on Proctor's behalf, but he is incapable of seeing through Abigail's rather obvious hypocrisy and evasion. Proctor understandably delays his own confession, hoping that Mary Warren's testimony will be sufficient to break the case against his wife. When he sees that Abigail is relentless and is about to destroy his witness, however, he attacks her and finally accuses her of lechery. But once again he has delayed too long, for he has already discredited himself in Danforth's eyes as an enemy of the court. When Abigail refuses to answer the charge, Danforth does not press her. Instead he calls in Elizabeth and asks her to testify. In a stunning reversal, Elizabeth lies to protect her husband, and Danforth eagerly accepts her word as proof of Proctor's deceit. Abigail leads the girls in an hysterical attack on Mary Warren who is terrified into turning against Proctor whom she accuses of being 'the Devil's man'. Finally enmeshed in the madness he could not overthrow, Proctor responds at first with anger, but then with insight.

I hear the boot of Lucifer, I see his filthy face! And it is my face, and yours, Danforth! For them that quail to bring men out of ignorance, as I have quailed, and as you quail now when you know in all your black hearts that this be fraud – God damns our kind especially, and we will burn, we will burn together!

This is the clearest evidence that Proctor comes to see himself as partly responsible for the evil that he has tried to condemn. Since he has just failed in one attempt to bring his fellow townsmen out of ignorance, he must here be referring to his initial reluctance to denounce the court as a fraud.

If the third act brings Proctor to a recognition of his complicity in the evil of Salem, the final act shows him coming to an acceptance of that guilt. Somewhat paradoxically, however, this act opens with Proctor at the lowest point in his spiritual development. He sits, reports the prison marshal, 'like some great bird; you'd not know he lived.' We are given no clue to Proctor's state of mind, but his subsequent appearance and his decision to confess suggest that he has lost all self-respect. From a reluctance to admit his own evil, he has come to complete self-loathing. His conviction that he is 'rotten' means that he lacks the pride necessary to maintain even the appearance of dignity. Somewhat characteristically, he looks outside for confirmation or denial of his worst fears. 'I would have your forgiveness', he says to his wife, hoping by securing it to reduce the load of guilt he feels. But Elizabeth realises what he himself does not yet comprehend, that her husband must learn to forgive himself. 'It come to naught that I should forgive you, if you'll not forgive yourself', she says. But she does admit that she may have been partially to blame. 'You take my sins upon you, John. . . . I never knew how I should say my love.'

Proctor's final quest is for some kind of truth that he can hold on to – a just evaluation of his life and of himself. As he refused to hand over his conscience to the court, he must not hand it over to his wife. But his sins against Elizabeth were real whereas the charges of Mary Warren were fraudulent. The inability of Proctor (or Miller) to draw clear distinctions between the two cases is one of the least satisfactory aspects of the play. The question of John's betrayal of Elizabeth seems to many to be sidetracked in the final moments of the play and lost sight of in the rather melodramatic 'victory' of Proctor's defiance of the court. The stricter moralists among the critics would deny that Proctor's courage in dying for his innocence of the charge of witchcraft in any way cancels out his guilt on the charge of adultery. Of course Miller would agree. The impression of moral confusion that seems to hang over the final moments of the play arises from the fact that the playwright is not interested in the question of Proctor's guilt (his guilt is taken for granted) so much as in Proctor's acceptance of that guilt.

At first Proctor is overwhelmed by a sense of worthlessness. He agrees to confess because he feels unworthy to be ranked with the saintly Rebecca and feels that such a confession could not corrupt him more. On the other hand he is reluctant to confess to the wrong sins. His refusal to name confederates and to have his confession publicised stems from the same cause – determination not to further the cause of the corrupt court. Although it seems that he is more jealous of his worldly reputation than of his credit with God, it is this last remnant of pride that saves him. The realisation that in the end he cannot publish a lie about himself convinces him that he is not as evil as he thought. In the shadow of the gallows he comes to realise that, if he is not as good a man as he once thought he was, neither is he entirely evil. Like most human beings, he is a mixture with not much more than 'a shred of goodness'. But his triumph in the end is that he is able to act out of that small virtue rather than succumbing to the despair that threatened to overcome him when he confronted his larger evil. When Elizabeth says, 'He have his goodness now,' she does not mean (as it might logically seem) that the venial John Proctor has been miraculously redeemed by the brave John Proctor. She means that he has found the true core of his nature which had been hidden beneath self-doubt and self-loathing.

The Crucible is a powerful play, eminently stageworthy, which has demonstrated repeatedly that it can have a very strong effect on an audience. Partly because of that power it is sometimes misunderstood. It has been seen as a criticism of the trial of accused spies Julius and Ethel Rosenberg, and as an attack on the House Committee on Un-American Activities. It has been dismissed as didactic melodrama, and praised as profound tragedy. It would be easy to attribute the confusion relating to the play to the political events surrounding its first production. But there are more fundamental reasons why the work continues to puzzle some readers and spectators. Foremost among these is the author's lack of complete objectivity. For while it is clear from Miller's comments, as well as from the text, that the playwright intends us to be critical of Proctor, it is practically impossible not to see him as a martyr. There are many reasons for this, not the least of which is Miller's rather ambivalent attitude to the central characters.

This ambivalence is particularly evident in the second-act scene between John and Elizabeth where Proctor's self-justification is uncommonly convincing. His rather sensual nature is revealed attractively through his discriminating taste for food, and his love of the sights and smells of the countryside. Elizabeth, by contrast, seems narrow and pinched in spirit: a bad cook, a forgetful wife, and a woman who does not even seem to take pleasure in flowers. Given these two personalities and the nature of their quarrel it is hard not to sympathise with Proctor and to start to see things from his point of view. He is so convincing in pleading his 'honesty' that we tend to overlook the fact that he is continually lying to his wife. Furthermore, Abigail is portrayed as such an obviously bad piece of goods that it takes a clear-eyed French critic to point out that Proctor was not only twice the age of the girl he seduced, but as her employer he was breaking a double trust. Furthermore, the extent of Abigail's sexual awakening suggests that before her affair with Proctor she was a virgin. Miller's decision to omit detailed references to the early stages of the rela-tionship has the effect of making Proctor's sense of guilt seem a little forced and perhaps not really justified.

A further difficulty some critics have with the play is what they see as its lack of religious dimension. It is perhaps inevitable that a twentieth-century author writing for twentieth-century audiences should portray the witch-scare in purely psychological and economic terms. But it is less understandable that Miller should fail to make some effort to show the support these Puritan martyrs gained from their faith. Apart from Rebecca and Elizabeth, none of the accused makes much reference to God. Indeed Proctor at the end is much more concerned about his 'name' than his soul. The fact that his actions will be judged in heaven by an all-seeing God, as well as in Salem by his very short-sighted neighbours, does not seem either to trouble or to comfort him.

Miller had been determined in *The Crucible* to empha-sise the tragic victory of the protagonist. This victory does not consist in the defeat of the court, but rather in Proctor's triumph over himself. At the end of the play, Proctor, like the Puritan martyrs of old, knows who he is. Whereas the strength of the original Salem victims came presumably from their faith in God, Proctor's will comes from his belief in himself. Rejecting the claims of his wife or society (and by implication religion) to judge him, he stands at the end on the judgement of the only tribunal he acknowledges, his own conscience. The problem with the play is that too many of the proceedings of that tribunal are held *in camera*.

6
A View from the Bridge

In spite of the growing popularity of his plays both in America and abroad in the early 1950s, Miller came increasingly to feel that he was being misunderstood. *Death of a Salesman*, which he had written half in 'laughter and joy', had been received as a work of the direst pessimism. When in his next play, Miller deliberately set out to create a more articulate hero, he had little more success in communicating his ideas. Not one reviewer of the original production of *The Crucible* mentioned what to Miller was the central theme of the work – the handing over of conscience to another. The sense of bewilderment and frustration resulting from this apparent incomprehension on the part of audiences and critics alike led Miller to make more explicit public statements about his aims as a playwright. In a series of essays, speeches and introductions to his plays published between 1949 and 1960, Miller expounded a comprehensive theory of drama which constitutes one of the most complete statements on the subject by a contemporary playwright. It would be pleasant if one could report that these essays have effectively dispelled all misunderstanding concerning Miller's work. Unfortunately that is far from the case. Indeed in some respects Miller's dramatic criticism serves only to complicate issues by emphasising the differences between what the playwright apparently intends to say and what in fact he does communicate. Few of his published statements are more confusing than the several explanations he has given for the writing and revision of *A View from the Bridge*.

In reflecting on the hostile criticism of *The Crucible* (much of which described the play as cold) Miller came to the conclusion that the implication that the play would have been improved by a greater emphasis on the subjective lives of the characters was wrong. What was needed, on the contrary, was not more subjectivism, but more self-awareness. The failure of modern realism to reveal more than the surface of life, Miller came to believe, was a result of the inability of playwrights and audiences to agree upon 'the pantheon of forces and values' which must lie behind that surface. In his next play, Miller resolved, he would transcend realism and create a form in which it would be possible to join feeling to awareness. Although he did not know what form such a drama would take, he felt that one model of the kind of wholeness he admired in drama was tragedy.

Tragedy can be described as an attempt to make some positive statement about human life in the face of defeat and death. It emerged in ancient Greece, and had a second flowering in the Renaissance, both periods of expansion and questioning after relatively more settled periods of faith. Tragedy addresses the problem of apparently unde-served suffering, and attempts to vindicate the claims of religion in the face of seeming injustice. The Greek answer (reflecting the Greek attitude to the gods) proclaims the power of fate and the weakness and blindness of man. In the tragic meeting between man and circumstance, man's error is acknowledged, but the emphasis is on external fate. In Aristotle's phrase, tragedy inspires in the spectator a mingling of 'pity' for the protagonist and 'terror' of the power and mystery of the gods.

Christian tragedies, such as those of Shakespeare, put greater emphasis on the human flaw. The suffering in Christian tragedy (often including the destruction of innocent bystanders such as Ophelia or Desdemona) is not the consequence of divine fiat, but of human passion or evil. As in Greek tragedy, the protagonist in Shakespeare must be removed before a healthy order can be restored. But because of the different emphasis, the catharsis in Christian tragedy is different. Pity for the protagonist is mixed with another emotion directed towards the heavens which is not so much terror as a kind of reverent dread. The sufferings of a Hamlet or a Lear are tolerable because they take place in a universe which is essentially understandable and moral.

The problem for the twentieth-century dramatist who would deal seriously with the most profound questions of life and death is that the background of reassurance once provided by religious faith no longer exists. In the face of almost universal scepticism few contemporary writers any longer attempt to present suffering as meaningful. Modern drama has tended on the whole to document man's frustration, defeat or despair, and to find its only significance in subjective experience. In a series of essays written after 1949, Miller attempted to formulate a theory of tragedy which would reintroduce the concept of 'victory' into drama.

His earliest pronouncements on the nature of tragedy appeared in the New York newspapers.[25] For Miller, the basic ingredients in tragedy are the protagonist's sense of indignation, and his compulsion to 'evaluate himself justly'. All the tragic heroes from Orestes to Macbeth, we are told, are destroyed in attempting to obtain their rightful place in society. What distinguishes the tragic hero from the mass of ordinary men is his willingness to question and attack the scheme of things that degrades him. This challenge of the seemingly stable cosmos produces terror in an audience which is fearful of being torn away from their image of what and who they are in the world. But it also enlightens. The spectacle of the hero's attack suggests an evil in his environment; his destruction hints at the existence of a moral law. The conflict in tragedy, therefore, is not between man and some irresistible fate; it shows the hero struggling against social forces that can be changed or overcome. For, as Miller says, tragedy must always show how the catastrophe might have been avoided, how good might have been allowed to express itself instead of succumbing to evil.

Miller's tragic aesthetic differs in many significant respects from traditional classical and Christian theories. In part, these differences can be traced to more recent ideas. For example, it owes a great deal to the Romantic celebration of heroes such as Satan, Prometheus and Faust. It owes something, too, to 'Ibsenism' as defined by George Bernard Shaw, and not a little to the social drama of the 1930s. But it is also a product of Miller's own exploration of dramatic form. In his plays from *The Man Who Had All the Luck* to *Death of a Salesman* Miller had been concerned with balancing defeat and victory. In *All My Sons* the narrow, family-centred morality of Joe Keller is replaced at the end of the play by the higher consciousness of Chris. In *Death of a Salesman*, Willy's belief in material success is transcended by Biff's self-fulfilment.

In planning the form of *A View from the Bridge*, Miller seems to have been determined that the 'generalized significance' of the play would be made plain to all. To ensure that his meaning could not be mistaken, he introduced a chorus figure who could address the audience directly. Characteristically *A View from the Bridge* is a two-level play in which the psychological and social elements seem sometimes at odds. Eddie Carbone, a longshoreman in the Red Hook district of Brooklyn, and his wife Beatrice have been responsible for the upbringing of their niece Catherine since the death of her parents when she was very young. Catherine is now seventeen, and Eddie's affection for her as a daughter has developed into something much more powerful without either Eddie or Catherine being aware of the change. Some hint of the possessive and unnatural form of his love is given by his reluctance to let Catherine wear high heels, but the full power of his passion does not emerge until Catherine wants to leave home to get married. At that point Eddie's jealousy brings him into direct and tragic conflict with his niece's boyfriend.

The social level of the play deals with the strict code of loyalty of the Sicilian–American community in which Eddie lives and with the tragic consequences of Eddie's infraction of that code. The crisis is precipitated by the arrival of Rodolpho and Marco, Beatrice's Italian relatives, who have been smuggled into the United States illegally. The Carbones take their relatives into their home where they provide them with food and shelter, but tensions between the visitors and their host build up quickly when it becomes apparent that Rodolpho and Catherine are beginning to fall in love. The antagonism reaches a climax when Eddie returns home early one day to find Rodolpho and Catherine in the bedroom. Eddie orders Rodolpho to leave whereupon Catherine starts to go with him. Eddie grasps her arm and says,

> You goin' with him. You goin' with him, heh? (*He grabs her face in the vise of his two hands.*) You goin' with him! (*He kisses her on the mouth as she pulls at his arms: he will not let go, keeps his face pressed against hers.*)[26]

Unable to admit the true nature of his feeling for Catherine, Eddie converts his jealousy of Rodolpho into a conviction that he is a homosexual and only interested in Catherine as a means of obtaining American citizenship. He appeals to Alfieri, the lawyer in the district, for a legal means of stopping what he has come to consider Rodolpho's theft of Catherine. Alfieri, sensing the true cause of Eddie's torment but unable to make him see it, tries to tell him that 'Somebody had to come for her . . . sooner or later.' He also warns Eddie against betraying Rodolpho to the immigration authorities, reminding him of the strict code against informers in the community.

> You won't have a friend in the world, Eddie! Even those who understand will turn against you.

Ignoring Alfieri's warning, Eddie phones the immigration officials who come and arrest Marco and Rodolpho as well as two other recently arrived immigrants. As he is led away, Marco spits in Eddie's face, and in front of his neighbours accuses him of betraying them.

The final scene shows Marco returning for vengeance. We are told that he has prayed in the church, but since he carries no weapon it is unclear whether he intends to kill Eddie or simply punish him with a beating. Waiting for Marco, Eddie refuses to run and tries once more to separate Rodolpho and Catherine. Beatrice begs him to release Catherine, saying of Rodolpho, 'It's her husband! Let her go.' When Catherine and Rodolpho start to leave,

> (*Eddie lunges and catches her: he holds her, and she weeps up into his face. And he kisses her on the lips.*)
> EDDIE: (*like a lover, out of his madness*)
>   It's me, ain't it?

When Marco finally arrives, Eddie accuses them of stealing Catherine from him and of making his name 'like a dirty rag'. 'I want my good name, Marco! You took my name!' Eddie pulls a knife, but Marco turns it on him, and he is fatally wounded. As he falls forward, he

> (*crawls a yard to Catherine. She raises her face away – but she does not move as he reaches over and grasps her leg, and looking up at her, he seems puzzled, questioning, betrayed.*)
> EDDIE: Catherine – why?

The play ends with a speech by Alfieri which presumably sums up Miller's understanding of the 'generalized significance' of the story as he has come to see it.

> Most of the time we settle for half,
> And I like it better.
> And yet, when the tide is right
> And the green smell of the sea
> Floats in through my window,
> The waves of this bay
> Are the waves against Siracusa.
> And I see a face that suddenly seems carved;

The eyes look like tunnels
Leading back toward some ancestral beach
Where all of us once lived.
And I wonder at those times
How much of all of us
Really lives there yet,
And when we will truly have moved on,
On and away from that dark place,
That world that has fallen to stones?

This version of the play seems to be a kind of Euripidean tragedy of passion in which the protagonist is overcome by an irresistible and self-destructive madness. The implication of the final speech is that such passion is essentially primitive, an aspect of human nature that belongs to a dead past, and that it is time that men moved on towards a more rational form of behaviour and society. But this implication is by no means clear and, within the context of the action of the play alone, Eddie seems to exhibit few of the qualities of the tragic protagonist as Miller had defined them in his essays.

This is all the more surprising since Miller had obviously been giving considerable thought to the nature of Greek drama during the writing of *A View from the Bridge*. His ideas are summed up in an essay entitled 'On Social Plays' which appeared as an introduction to the published version of the play a couple of months after the Broadway opening. Here he describes the wholeness of Greek drama which he feels has been lost on the modern stage, and discusses a new form of social drama which he feels might recapture the Greek breadth of vision.

The principal way in which classical drama differs from modern plays, Miller feels, is in its concern with ultimate law. The Greek dramatist was interested in psychology, but only as a means to a larger end which was the discovery of the Grand Design, the right way to live together. The grandeur of Greek drama was its ability to treat both the private life *and* the social context. 'For when the Greek thought of the right way to live it was a whole concept, it meant a way to live that would create citizens who were brave in war, had a sense of responsibility to the polis [city state] in peace, and were also developed as individual personalities.'[27]

Modern drama, Miller thinks, has lost the ability to deal with the whole man. The 'social drama' from Ibsen and Shaw to the left-wing playwrights of the 1930s has put too much emphasis on social causation. On the other hand, the 'psychological drama' is often nothing more than a purely private examination of individuality for the sake of the examination or for art's sake. What is needed is a new social drama which will combine the approach of the Greek theatre with modern discoveries in psychology and economics.

In this essay Miller is clearly addressing problems related to the writing of a modern tragedy such as *A View from the Bridge*. The dilemma facing the modern dramatist is twofold says Miller: first, we no longer believe that some ultimate sense can be made of social causation, and second, no single individual can any longer be considered representative of a whole people. How then does the contemporary playwright portray the kind of tragic figure who would have the power to pass over the boundary of the known social law in order to discover a way of life which would yield excellence? Miller's solution in the first version of *A View from the Bridge* was to create an objective narrator who could see and describe the larger context which was hidden from the hero, and to write about a relatively closed society in which the conflict between the protagonist and the social law would engage the passions of the whole community.

There is some evidence that even before the production of the play, Miller may have been dissatisfied with the solutions he attempted in it. A central problem was his inability to grasp what he felt to be the ultimate meaning of the story. When he first heard the tale from a waterfront worker in Brooklyn, he felt that the weaving together of the lives of the characters seemed almost the work of fate. But in dramatising it he had been unable to define the objective and subjective elements that made that fate. Consequently he felt that a certain mystery remained that he could not account for.

During the rehearsals for the production, Miller and the director, Martin Ritt, strove to achieve a non-naturalistic style of acting and design which would encourage a more objective response, so that the audience's emotional identification with Eddie would not overwhelm their ability to judge his actions in the social context. To this end, excessive and arbitrary gestures were eliminated, the set was designed to be suggestive of the classical parallels Miller saw in the story. The problem was that neither the director (a former member of the Group Theatre) nor the actors had any experience with this kind of staging. The result was not a success.

Brooks Atkinson of the *New York Times* probably reflected the general reaction when he criticised the very effects Miller and Ritt had used to distance the audience. 'Mr. Miller's principle of underwriting', he wrote, 'may have been ill-advised . . . . Eddie's deficiency as a tragic hero is simply that Miller has not told us enough about him.' Atkinson went on to say that far from being a 'hero' Eddie seemed mean and vicious, and got just about what he deserved. The characters of the wife and niece were also

1. *All My Sons*, New York, 1947

2a. *Death of a Salesman*, New York, 1949: Lee J. Cobb as Willy Loman

2b. *Death of a Salesman*, London, 1949: Jo Mielziner's set

3.   *Death of a Salesman*, London, 1949: Willy Loman's Family mourning his death

4.   *The Crucible*, New York, 1953

5. *The Crucible*, Bristol Old Vic Company, 1954

6a. The set of *A View From the Bridge*, New York, 1956

6b. *A View From the Bridge*, London, 1956: Mary Ure and Anthony Quayle

7.   *The Creation of the World*, New York, 1972

8. *Death of a Salesman*, London, 1980: Warren Mitchell as Willy Loman

criticised for being too sketchy. The actors seemed to portray abstract ideas rather than human beings, and the performance reminded Atkinson of the style of the Group Theatre 'all mind and nerves' and no flesh.[28]

A second circumstance that made Miller dissatisfied with the first version of the play was his discovery of his own personal connection with it. After seeing the production several times, he suddenly realised that the piece was in some part an analogy to situations in his own life. What those situations were Miller never explained. Perhaps he saw in Eddie's infatuation for Catherine a parallel to his own interest in Marilyn Monroe. Possibly he came to think that his total condemnation of Eddie the informer was simplistic in view of the inroads passion had made in his own life? Whatever the nature of the new insights Miller had into the story, when the opportunity arose to have the play produced in London, he felt he had to rewrite it to include them.

In the revised play, the characters of Beatrice and Catherine were considerably enlarged, and they played a more direct role in Eddie's fate. Furthermore the London production was conceived in a much more realistic mode. The set was a highly detailed reconstruction of the Brooklyn apartment with its surroundings of alleys and fire-escapes, and most of the poetry of the first version was eliminated or the ideas expressed in the vivid Brooklyn argot of the neighbourhood. The classically trained British actors were better able than their American counterparts to find an acting style that would move easily from the highly emotional to the sedately dignified.

Even more interesting than the alterations in form, however, are the changes Miller made in the central character. In this revised version, Miller plays down Eddie's physical passion for Catherine and focuses instead on his relationship to Marco. In the concluding minutes of the play it is Marco's insult, not Rodolpho's rivalry, which is foremost in Eddie's mind. When Beatrice attempts to make him confront his real motive, Eddie turns away from the truth.

> BEATRICE: Who could give you your name? . . . if [Marco] goes on his knees, what is he got to give you? That's not what you want.
>
> EDDIE: Don't bother me!
>
> BEATRICE: You want something else, Eddie, and you can never have her! . . . The truth is not as bad as blood, Eddie! I'm tellin' you the truth – tell her good-by forever.[29]

Confronted with this truth, however, Eddie cannot accept it and cries out his repudiation, 'That's what you think of me – that I could have such a thought?' When he goes out to challenge Marco shouting 'I want my name,' therefore, he is persisting in a deluded course of action. Eddie's concern with his 'name', though superficially similar to John Proctor's at the end of *The Crucible*, is in reality very different. Whereas Proctor comes to see that his name is something only he can evaluate justly, Eddie believes falsely his name is in the custody of his accusers. In the revised version, Eddie dies in the arms of Beatrice, and Miller probably intends to suggest by this that he finally comes to some kind of acceptance of his nature and his strange love.

Alfieri's final speech in the two-act version is very different from the original. Paradoxically the emphasis seems to shift away from the universal and primitive nature of Eddie's passion to the unique qualities of the man.

Most of the time now we settle for half and I like it better. But the truth is holy, and even as I know how wrong he was, and his death useless, I tremble, for I confess that something perversely pure calls to me from his memory – not purely good, but himself purely, for he allowed himself to be wholly known and for that I will love him more than all my sensible clients. And yet, it is better to settle for half, it must be! And so I mourn him – I admit it – with a certain . . . alarm.

The relationship of all this to the play and to Eddie's character seems to me to be extremely obscure. Alfieri is contrasting the sensible people who settle for half and the potentially tragic individuals who cannot let well enough alone. According to Miller's theory of tragedy, such individuals are driven to act when others would retire, and in so acting they cause the scheme of things to act with retributive violence against them. But in what way can Eddie's actions be interpreted as a challenge of the 'stable cosmos' and how do they lead to the discovery of new understanding or a moral law? What 'holy truth' has been pursued by this protagonist or revealed by his death?

Superficially it would seem that the evil in this play is not in the environment, but in Eddie, and in this respect the play is fairly traditional. In the revised version of the play, however, Miller has introduced lines to suggest that he is contrasting the Sicilian–American code of revenge with Beatrice's plea for forgiveness, and that he intends to imply that the tragedy would not have happened if Eddie had acknowledged the dark side of his nature. But these themes (if indeed they are implicit) are overshadowed by the spectacle of Eddie's slide into madness. The strangely inappropriate nature of Alfieri's concluding comment suggests that Miller has still not fathomed the mystery at the centre of this story, and that its meaning still eludes him.

An opportunity to try for a third time to come to grips with the story of Eddie Carbone arose during the rehearsals for the Paris production. The director, Peter Brook, was apparently informed that no French audience would accept the notion that Eddie and Catherine could be unaware of the nature of the love between them. For this production, therefore, Miller wrote a third ending in which Marco refuses to kill Eddie. Isolated by his neighbours who make him realise that he himself is responsible for the loss of his good name, Eddie kills himself.[30] This ending seems in many ways the most intellectually satisfying, although it is perhaps psychologically improbable.

When he was preparing his plays for the collected edition of his dramatic works, it was the London version of *A View from the Bridge* that he selected to be printed. In the introduction to his *Collected Plays*, Miller returned again to a consideration of the play and what he had learned from the two very different productions. His original conception of the character of Eddie had been, he felt, too objective. In revising the play he found it possible to identify much more fully with Eddie and to make him more sympathetic to the audience. This made it more possible to mourn a man who, although guilty of the most serious offences, nevertheless had a certain dignity. Even more important than the insight into Eddie's character, however, were the lessons Miller learned about dramatic form. By comparing the reception of the play in London and New York he became convinced that the ultimate test of a play's effectiveness was performance in the theatre. 'A play', he wrote, 'ought to make sense to common-sense people . . . . It is their innate conservatism which, I think, is and ought to be the barrier to excess in experiment and the exploitation of the bizarre'.[31] Miller's choice of the second version of *A View from the Bridge* for inclusion in his *Collected Plays* suggests a repudiation of the 'distancing' effects he had experimented with at first. He became convinced that 'the theater is above all else an instrument of passion.' To create new forms, requires greater attention, not less, to the 'inexorable, common, pervasive conditions of existence'.[32]

7
Non-Theatrical Writing

In the plays following *Death of a Salesman* Miller has tried in a variety of ways to overcome what he felt was a certain lack of comprehension on the part of his audience. His failure to find a form that would illuminate the issues that he saw underlying the events he dramatised led him to a period of self-doubt. He began to feel that in the works he had written for Broadway he had been little more than a 'kind of entertainer succeeding in drawing a tear or a laugh . . . [but that] what was behind his plays remained a secret.'[33] During the eight years or so that separated the London production of *A View from the Bridge* and the New York première of *After the Fall*, Miller continued to look for a way to unite in his drama the 'pervasive conditions of existence' with the 'hidden' laws that gave significance to that existence. But his efforts were disappointing and he found himself turning increasingly to non-dramatic forms, especially the short story. Miller had written reportage and fiction in the early 1940s, but during the period 1956–60 he was to find in the short story what almost amounts to a new voice. Quieter in tone, more intimate, less desperate in their striving after meaning, Miller's stories constitute a neglected aspect of his work. In his fiction we can see the author dealing with the ideas that concern him in his plays, but his treatment of these ideas is more subtle.

Such subtlety did not come immediately. In his first prose works we can see all too plainly the assumptions that underlie his early plays. *Situation Normal* (1944) is an account of Miller's investigation of American training bases undertaken as background for the screenplay of *The Story of G.I. Joe.* It is a series of vivid sketches of officers and enlisted men interspersed with reflections by the author which reveal little about the American fighting man, but a great deal about the young Arthur Miller. It is clear that Miller was anything but objective as a reporter. Because he himself saw the war so clearly as a crusade against fascism in defence of democracy and the principle of equality, he wanted the American soldiers to see it in the same light. But he had to admit that they did not. 'It is terrible to me that everything is so personal. . . . I can't seem to find men who betray a social responsibility as a reason for doing or not doing anything.'[34] Because of his own convictions, however, Miller could not accept the evidence of his senses. So he attributed to the men a kind of subconscious understanding of the war which they could not express. 'I am beginning to think that perhaps those beliefs are there in a totally unsuspected guise.' Some justification for this hope was supplied by a veteran soldier by the name of Watson who was failing his officer's training course because of a sense of disorientation after combat. Explaining the pressures of battle, Watson said,

You find out all about yourself out there, as if all the excuses you've always made for yourself were suddenly very silly. Friendship is the greatest thing out there. . . . I tell you the truth: I would die for any one of thirty or forty men out there just as easy as I'd flick out this match.

Miller magnified this sense of loyalty and unit pride into something more mystical. 'No man', he claims, 'has ever felt identity with a group more deeply and intimately than a soldier in battle.' In that state, Miller suggests, there is complete equality, a common aim, no little prejudices or selfish aims, and everyone gains a sense of 'exhilaration' from the knowledge that he is helping an enormous mass of men toward a great and worthy goal. The kind of purposeful and unified society produced by danger, he feels, can also be created by a 'commonality of Belief'. The sceptical might reflect that this vision of common purpose perhaps owes as much to socialist idealism as it does to direct observation, but there is no doubt that it was an important part of Miller's belief at the time.

The second conviction was his sense that without a clear idea of why he had fought and what he had accomplished, the returning American veteran would become a prey to the destructive tendencies in American life. Opposed to the ideal of community in the foxholes, Miller saw the evil of a society of selfish competition in which each person tries to exclude his neighbours. In such a society, unless the returning soldier's attachment to his home was overwhelming, 'he was going to feel the loss of a social unit . . . a social goal worth his sacrifice'. The only thing which could rejoin the soldier with America was a 'Belief in the rightness, the justness, the necessity of his fight' which he could share with all civilians. Without such a belief, Miller feared, the returning soldier would be lost, restless, and an easy prey to demagogues.

It is interesting in this connection that Miller does not

present the family as the kind of unit that can give significance and purpose to life. Quite the contrary. In most cases, Miller feels, the family represents an obstacle to the kind of social solidarity he sees as the ideal. Too often, the home is inward-looking, concerned with its own selfish welfare rather than with that of the larger social group. It is significant too that, although he does not say so explicitly, Miller implies that this narrowness is a result of the women who cannot comprehend the larger issues and loyalties brought out by war. The book ends in a characteristically ambiguous way with a young combat veteran trying to talk to his girlfriend. 'He suffers for her and for his inability to know what it really is he wants her to feel. He recalls how easy it was to talk to the guys in the squadron, how simple to communicate without talking at all.'

In his second major prose work, the novel *Focus* (1945), Miller addresses the questions of belief and communication in a different context. The activities of the Christian Front, a violently anti-Semitic group which became active in New York towards the end of the war, seemed to confirm Miller's fears that individuals without an understanding of why the war had been fought were susceptible to antisocial demagogy. Miller was interested in tracing the process by which an individual might move from blindness to understanding. *Focus* deals with the awakening of social conscience in a gentile when he suddenly experiences for himself the effects of anti-Semitism. Lawrence Newman is a personnel officer in a large New York office who is responsible for enforcing the company policy against hiring Jews. When he buys himself a badly needed pair of glasses he begins to be taken for a Jew himself, and when the supervisor tries to move him to a less conspicuous office he resigns in indignation. He is finally taken on by a Jewish firm where he encounters a woman he had previously refused to hire on the mistaken assumption that she was Jewish. Seeing her now in an entirely different light he falls in love with her and marries her. Following his purchase of glasses, and increasingly after his marriage, Newman is subjected to pressures to join a movement to force a Jewish merchant away from the Brooklyn neighbourhood in which Newman lives. Prompted by his wife who realises that they must either join with the Christian Front or be attacked by it, Newman attends a Front rally. There he is mistaken for a Jew and thrown out. A couple of nights later, in the company of his wife, he is attacked by a group of young toughs. The attack coincides with an attack on the Jewish merchant, and Newman and Finklestein find themselves fighting side by side until they finally drive off their assailants. Newman reports the attack to the police who also mistake him for a Jew. Realising at last the true brotherhood of man, he allows the mistake to go uncorrected.

The novel is rather too contrived to be entirely believable psychologically. The metamorphosis of Newman is a clever technical device to emphasise the superficiality of the causes of prejudice, and the unreliability of sight as a means of knowing someone. The early cautious and apprehensive Newman is especially well drawn, but it seems improbable that such a man could become transformed into the resolute fighter of the second half of the novel. Characteristically Miller introduces sex as an important subsidiary theme, but the story of Newman's courtship and marriage is not fully explored, nor is its relevance to the main theme at all clear. Nevertheless, *Focus* is an extremely interesting work for what it reveals about certain fundamental political and psychological assumptions of the author.

Underlying the title and the central image of the

spectacles is the belief that people do not really see one
another. Newman comes to understand Finklestein as a
man (rather than as a stereotype) as a result of two
incidents. First he shares Finklestein's experience when he
himself suffers from anti-Semitism. But more important,
he is made to understand the Jew when Finklestein turns on
him in anger.

> Standing there looking into his angry face, Newman's
> idea of him altered. Where once he had seen a rather
> comical, ugly, and obsequious face, now he found a man,
> a man throbbing with anger. And somehow his anger
> made him comprehensible to Mr. Newman.[35]

I'm not sure that this is believable psychology, but it is
closely related to Miller's fervent conviction that no man
should allow himself to be victimised. There is a recurring
refusal on the part of Miller's characters to accept without
question the outside world's assessment of their character
or motives. This refusal arises from the need these characters feel to justify or explain themselves (or, as Miller
expresses it, to 'evaluate themselves justly'). Although
Miller sees this characteristic as a universal human need,
felt most strongly by the tragic hero, it seems more likely to
be the experience of a member of a minority group facing
the prejudice or indifference of the majority.

The vital necessity of rebelling against stereotyping is
illustrated in the novel by the story of Itzik the pedlar. The
story is recounted by Finklestein who heard it from his
father and concerns a peasant rebellion on a repressive
estate in nineteenth-century Poland. When the Baron
owner of the estate returns after one of his absences, he
finds his overseers dead, his house ransacked and his
money stolen. Discovering that the peasants do not know

the nature of money and have mistaken the paper bills for pictures, he rides into the neighbouring village and commands Itzik (who had never before been allowed to trade on the estate) to go and sell wares to the peasants. When Itzik discovers the wealth that the peasants have unknowingly acquired, he is filled with apprehension, but nevertheless exchanges his goods for the money and arrives home that evening with more than a million kroner in a bag. At night soldiers come. They destroy Itzik's house, kill his children and club the pedlar into unconsciousness. The next day Itzik awakes to see the Baron ride up to the house, take the money and leave. When asked what the story meant, Finklestein's father had always said it meant nothing, that Itzik was powerless to prevent it from happening and had no choice but to go along with circumstances. But his son refuses to accept that meaning. He sees that 'Itzik should never have allowed himself to accept a role that was not his, a role that the baron had created for him. . . . he should have allowed his indignation to carry him away and gotten on his wagon and driven directly home.' According to Finklestein, Itzik was unable to resist the soldiers during the pogrom because he was weakened by his sense of guilt for having taken the money.

The function of the story in the novel is clear. It is a parable about the dangers of non-resistance. Significantly, resistance takes two forms. The initial, and most important, resistance is against being cast in a false role. Itzik's refusal to trade with the peasants would not have affected the outcome of the story, but it would have preserved his dignity and enabled him to fight the soldiers with a clear conscience. For Miller, one of the greatest obstacles to perceiving and pursuing the good is fear. And fear is frequently a product of guilt. Newman's ignorance and fear are related. The novel begins with his fearing to go to the aid of a woman being attacked outside his house. It ends with him no longer afraid because he at last understands the nature of prejudice. From being a victim of forces he does not understand, he becomes a free agent able to choose his destiny.

A peculiarity of these early works is the essentially masculine nature of the communal ideal. In both prose works the male world of action, sacrifice and loyalty is contrasted with the female world of subjectivity, timidity and selfishness. Although Gertrude in *Focus* embodies a number of female characteristics (few of them attractive), it is her final desertion of Newman when the latter is being attacked that is most significant. In Miller's terms, her lack of physical courage is a symbol, not a cause, of her 'sin' of incomprehension. In his later work Miller comes to realise that his earlier views had been rather too simplistic. But until very late, his vision of the world reflects some curious anti-feminine biases.

An interesting transitional work in which the ideal of male comradeship is held up for scrutiny is 'The Misfits', a short story written in 1957 about his experiences in Nevada when he spent six weeks there prior to filing for divorce. In the story, Gay Langland, Perce Howland and Guido Racanelli are three itinerant cowboys who make a living at a variety of odd jobs. As the tale opens they are working respectively as a gigolo, a rodeo rider and a garage mechanic. But these occupations are temporary. The work that gives Gay and Guido the most satisfaction, and the labour by which they choose to define themselves, is the hunting of wild mustangs. Once an honourable occupation needed to supply riding ponies and breeding stock for the farms and ranches in the region, the hunt has degenerated into a sordid pursuit of the small remnants of the once vast herds for sale to the processors of dogfood. The three men view the hunt differently. Guido, a callous veteran of many bombing missions during the Second World War, takes pride in the technical aspects of the hunt – the pursuit by plane and truck, and the use of heavy tyres to capture the horses – all of which are his inventions. Gay rather stolidly persists in the enterprise maintaining that what he is doing has not changed, but that society has demeaned his labour. Perce, the youngest, is the only one to respond to the suffering of the horses themselves, or to perceive any tragedy in their destruction. But they all agree that the hunt is 'better than wages', and somehow convince themselves that it represents an honourable alternative to enslavement by a commercial society. In the end, Perce's scruples are quelled as he agrees to accompany the others to Thighbone Mountain to ferret out the last survivors of the wild herds.

Miller's portrayal of this pathetic group of 'misfits' is brilliantly ambiguous. On the one hand, they represent the last of a dying breed of men whose courage and spirit of independence recall the days of the American frontier. Huge as it was, that frontier had a sense of community and common purpose which had even then been destroyed in other parts of America. In the west the community transcended family. It was an 'endless range . . . and it connected [a man] sufficiently with his father and his wife and his children. . . . [Gay felt that] he had neither left anyone nor not-left as long as they were all alive on those ranges.'[36] In such a world, family life is pleasant (Gay remembers his home as the best part of his life), but it is essentially limiting – 'a stake to which [one is] pleasurably tethered'. On the other hand, Miller shows with a restrained irony the limitations of these 'heroes'. None of the men is capable of seeing his actions as having any larger significance. Since the death of his wife and baby, Guido has lost his ability to love, and the sense of 'loose gaiety' he feels is a symptom of his lack of sense of purpose. Gay is immature, with boyish facial features and an adolescent's need to do things which he cannot explain or justify logically. Perce is also young with a young man's sensitivity, but totally lacking in ambition and will-power. These men have refused to accept the conventional role of wage-earner that American society attempts to impose on its members. But unlike Itzik, unlike Newman and Finklestein, they have not found their dignity. Instead they have themselves become victimisers, enslaving and destroying the mustangs to avoid enslavement by the capitalist system.

Miller's balance of sympathy in 'The Misfits' is evidence of a much more complex understanding of the problem of individual integrity. It is true that the men's work has been turned to corrupt ends by a commercial society, but is there not something in the men that has collaborated in that corruption? Are the cowboys trapped or free? The story ends with a long and detailed description of the captured horses. The adults stand roped to the heavy tyres, helplessly awaiting their fate.

> From time to time the stallion caught the smell of the pastures [in the mountains] and he started to walk toward the vaulted fields in which he had grazed; but the tire bent his neck around, and after a few steps he would turn to face it and leap into the air with his forelegs striking at the sky, and then he would come down and be still again.

The 'misfit' horses are obviously a symbol of the misfit men, and the image of their helplessness is both pitiable and outrageous. But there is one horse, the colt, which is unfettered and confined only by something in its nature. On the way back to town Gay asks Perce if he is going to

101

join him on the hunt in Thighbone Mountain. 'Okay,' Perce says and goes back to sleep. In a symbolically parallel situation, the colt, although free to leave the captured mare, does not.

> When the first pink glow of another morning lit the sky the colt stood up, and as it had always done at dawn it walked waywardly for water. The mare shifted and her bone hoofs ticked the clay. The colt turned its head and returned to her and stood at her side with vacant eye, its nostrils sniffing the warming air.

'The Misfits' constitutes a sombre picture of man's relationship to society in that it recognises the relentless power of inner forces working against freedom and self-realisation. In this story, belief and knowledge are not enough if they are unsupported by sensitivity and will.

An interesting development of Miller's perceptions about the origins of alienation is to be found in the story 'I Don't Need You Any More' (1959). This is a sensitive account of a young Jewish boy's ambivalent feelings towards his family on the last day of a seaside holiday. The piece undoubtedly draws heavily on Miller's recollections of his own childhood, and is one of the few extended accounts of his memories of that time before the 'fall' of 1929. The story is told from the point of view of its five-year-old protagonist, Martin. The action takes place during Yom Kippur, and recounts the contradictory emotions of a young boy as he stands between childhood and manhood. The central incident involves Martin's retaliation against what he senses as his mother's withdrawal of love. In a moment of anger he strikes out at her, shouting, 'I don't need you any more.' This and subsequent outbursts of childish violence disturb the holiday atmosphere and provoke short-lived tensions in the relationships of his parents and brother.

A marked characteristic of the story, and an obstacle to simple interpretation, is the intense, almost hallucinatory nature of the boy's experience. A somewhat out-of-focus perspective is partly the result of Martin's youth and imperfect understanding. His father and older brother have gone to the synagogue, leaving him at home with his mother, where he feels a sense of frustration at this exclusion from the adult male world of sacrifice (it is a fast day), responsibility and understanding. His previously close relationship with his mother has also altered as a result of her pregnancy and his gradual exclusion from his parents' bedroom as he approaches an age of sexual awareness. Martin senses this alteration of his position in the family, but his understanding of what is happening is distorted by his hyperactive imagination. Once an infallible means of winning astonishment and approval, his story-telling ability has also begun to fail him recently as he detects clearer and clearer evidence of a lack of interest or even belief on the part of his listeners. Now he begins to see that his own experiences do not correspond with those of his parents and brother. There are certain things which cannot be told without unpredictable consequences.

The first information Martin acquires that he knows he must keep to himself is the fact that his mother almost married someone other than his father. The knowledge that his family is not eternal, that his mother and father do not have absolutely inseparable lives, seems to Martin a terrible burden which he must guard in order to protect them. Another secret he cannot impart to the others is his vision of God, who he perceives to be in the ocean along with the bearded sins which have been shed on the day of atonement.

Like much of Miller's work, 'I Don't Need You Any More'

is a study of alienation. Whereas previously the author had tended to regard antisocial behaviour as something contrary to natural human inclination, here he shows separateness to be the product of awareness. Martin's alienation is only partly a matter of choice. It is true that he repudiates his need for (and therefore connection with) his mother, and deliberately chooses a path that will take him away from his family into the world of sin and knowledge (the sea 'where he belongs'). But that course is also partially determined for him. It is, Miller seems to suggest, an inevitable concomitant of growing up and even of language itself. At one point in the story when Martin strives to repeat his claim to independence, his tongue refuses to work and he is left speechless. In that state he acquires

> a smoothed-out view that was cleared of the necessity to be thinking at every instant what he should or should not say next. . . . Beauty seemed to be forming around him, all of them gently rising and falling together in an imminence. . . . The fact was spreading through his mind that this was a wonder . . . . They were all sharing the single belief together, and this sudden unity, fusing them without warning, burned away his sense of having secrets. . . . in this moment there was no Mama or Papa or Ben but three congealments of warmth embracing him with no thoughts of their own. And it seemed to him now that this was all he had been trying to find, this was actual and perfect, while everything else, the whole past of arguments and fights and smiles and shouts, was a dream.[37]

This almost mystical intuition of unity is only momentary, however, and when he finds his voice again, Martin recreates the world of discreteness. He finds himself suddenly the cause of argument between his parents, and later of hostility in his brother, and he realises dimly that it is the feeling of oneness which is illusory. That night he goes down to the beach where he experiences what is almost a religious call.

> He yearned to know what he should do for God . . . . He now vowed obedience to the sea, the moon, the starry beach and the sky, and the silence that stretched its emptiness all around him. What exactly its command was he did not know, but an order was coming to him from the night, . . . and it made him better and no longer quite alone. He felt . . . he was the guardian of Ben's and his parents' innocence. Vaguely he felt that with some words which he knew were somewhere in his head he had almost sent them all screaming and roaring at one another and at him, so that – had he said what he could say, they would all be horrified at the mere sight of one another and there would be a terror of crashing. He must keep them from that knowledge . . . . In league with rule, in charge of the troubled peace, he slept in the strength of his ministry.

What is interesting about this account of an artist's awakening sense of his vocation is the apparently paradoxical emphasis it puts on silence. Whereas previously Miller had shown the writer as a bearer of healing truth, here he recognises that an artist's secret knowledge can be destructive. The promise that some kind of purposeful collectivity was possible seemed a gospel that everyone would welcome. But if such a hope were illusory, or if it should be possible only on the sub-verbal or infantile level, then how should the writer communicate such frightening news?

Miller's exploration of some of these ideas is carried still further in the screen adaptation of 'The Misfits' which he wrote as a vehicle for his wife, Marilyn Monroe. In expanding the short story Miller faced several problems. The formal requirements of film demanded greater development in plot and character. To provide these he dramatised many incidents preceding the mustang hunt. He also enlarged the part of Roslyn and introduced her into the final scenes of the film where her presence required a complete revision of the ending. The resolution of the story gave Miller considerable trouble, and he worked on it right up to the last day of shooting. The ending finally settled on is not wholly satisfying and betrays a certain unsureness on the author's part.

Another problem with the film is the tendency of the visual images to submerge, or even obscure altogether, the writer's feelings about certain subjects. The most obvious example is the final sequence showing the mustang hunt. This is so strong visually, and so obviously cruel and senseless, that it is difficult for many viewers to see anything at all heroic in the cowboys' activity. And yet we must feel sympathetic to the men if we are to have the necessary respect for Gay's former life. There are other examples, too, where what Miller calls the 'effect of documentation inevitable in photography' is inadequate to convey the meanings which Miller spelled out for the readers of the published version of the script. The shots in the film of the Dayton crowds, for example, do not unequivocally convey the impression of a society 'enslaved by its own will' as Miller describes it in the printed version. Possibly because of the neutrality of many of the photographic images (or perhaps because of the mass audience to which the film was directed), Miller has written dialogue which is much more explicit, much more naively 'significant' than any of his stage speech. The result is a curious sentimentality (even banality) which is not to be found in his plays and stories.

Part of the uncertainty one senses in the film may be due to the fact that here Miller is in very unfamiliar territory. Not only was he inexperienced in the medium, but *The Misfits* is one of the playwright's few explorations of romantic love, and the only work in which it is a major theme. Roslyn's invasion of the all-male world of the three cowboys has the effect of challenging and upsetting many of their assumptions. Gay, the chief representative of this world of action and purpose, comes into direct conflict with Roslyn and (for the first time in Miller's work) it is the instinctive and 'domestic' values rather than the intellectual and public ones which triumph. Gay says,

> I never bothered to battle a woman before. And it was peaceful, but a lot like huggin' the air. This time I thought I'd lay my hand on the air again – but it feels like I touched the whole world. I bless you girl.[38]

Whereas in the story Gay continues to pursue his illusory notion of self-sufficiency and heroic action, in the film he is brought to see that he has been 'roping a dream'. The agent of his conversion is Roslyn who represents a kind of 'knowing' very different from the cowboys' blinkered conviction that anything is 'better than wages'. What Gay learns from Roslyn in the film is an openness to life and a hope for the future which his counterpart in the story never acquires.

If this 'domestication' of Gay Langland constitutes one action of the film, a secondary theme is the education of Roslyn Tabor. Here, it seems to me, Miller is not at the top of his form. Roslyn is less a character of flesh and blood than a product of a romantic imagination (considerably stimulated, it is true, by the personality of Marilyn Monroe). Roslyn has left her first husband because, as she says, 'he was not *there*.' This failure of communication in her first marriage is not examined or explained, and it is not entirely obvious why she is so lonely and afraid to depend on anyone. The quality in her which attracts the three men (apart from her natural physical charms) is a spontaneous sympathy and hopefulness which Guido defines as 'a gift for life'. Each of the cowboys falls in love with her, but it is Gay who gives her the strength she seems to need. He does this in part by his care for her, but also by encouraging her to face the unpleasant realities of life. He tries to make her see the reasonableness of hunting, and to understand that a kind man can kill. By the end of the story she seems ready to 'take a little bad with the good' and to stop running away. In the final scene she envisages a world without fear in a child (presumably combining her sensitivity and Gay's courage) who could be 'brave from the beginning'.

The film of *The Misfits* fails because Miller seems to be seeing some of his old ideas in a new light and wrestling (still unsuccessfully) with some new themes. Gay, like Joe Keller, Willy Loman and Eddie Carbone, has a glorified and self-deceiving notion of himself and of the significance of his actions. Earlier Miller heroes could not, or would not, face the truth about themselves and became victims of despair or wilful blindness. Gay, on the other hand, faces the truth, but makes up his own mind about how to confront it. When he releases the stallion, he does so, not as a victim, or an individual accepting a role, but as a free agent. Just what Gay's future will hold is not certain. Guido's taunt that nothing remains for Gay now but a life of wage-earning at some gas station or laundromat may not be far from the truth, but seems hardly what Miller intends to suggest as a better means for Gay to 'prove he is alive'. Possibly Guido's unfinished house between the selfish lawless society of the city and the 'dream' of the frontier life is what lies at the end of the highway under the stars at the end of the film. One feels, however, that the playwright has not really worked out the implications of his rather mawkish conclusion.

The most interesting character thematically is Roslyn. On one level she represents a new celebration of instinct over abstraction. The elevation of the feminine qualities of subjectivity and empathy to a level equal to male courage and deliberation is something new in Miller. Equally new is the recognition that the life of companionship in a unified purpose may not be as innocent as Miller once believed. The corruption of Gay's hunting or Roslyn's dancing may have been caused by society, but the individual is nevertheless free to walk away from that corruption. The problems raised by the coexistence of kindness and cruelty are not resolved in *The Misfits*. A deeper exploration of these problems was to be at the heart of Miller's next stage play.

8
After the Fall

After the Fall is Miller's most experimental, subtle and profound work. It is a culmination of his many earlier attempts to combine detailed psychological portraiture with a criticism of society and a search for ultimate meaning. In his determination to get as close to 'reality' as possible, Miller has gone inside the head of his protagonist to dramatise Quentin's subjective life. In the process, the objective world virtually disappears to be replaced by a fluid, timeless 'consciousness' into which memories come and go at the prompting of will or passion. The story of the play, therefore, is not concerned with Quentin's actions in the world, but with his inner search for some pattern in his existence, some 'law' that would explain the disaster of his life.

Because of the nature of this search, the figures in Quentin's recollections are both vividly individualised and at the same time mythic. Quentin is partly Arthur Miller painfully reviewing incidents in his own mental and emotional development; but he is also Everyman looking for a

110

way to survive with dignity in the modern world; he is Cain wandering in the desert. In the same way, Louise and Maggie bear certain resemblances to Miller's first two wives, but they also embody opposing attitudes to sex that can be said to go to the roots of the western Judaic–Hellenistic tradition. Because of the complexity of the work and the seemingly sensational nature of its revelations, *After the Fall* was given a very mixed reception when it first opened early in 1964.

That opening seemed at the time singularly propitious. The play not only marked the beginning of the Repertory Theater of Lincoln Center, it brought together for the first time since *Salesman* the theatrical talents of Miller, Elia Kazan and Jo Mielziner. By general agreement the collaboration did not repeat its triumph of some fifteen years earlier. The scenic problems presented by the script and the auditorium proved insurmountable. The large open stage and wide amphitheatre of the ANTA–Washington Square Theatre was better suited to large epic productions than to the intimate and subtle requirements of *After the Fall*. Miller wanted to create a theatrical equivalent for the 'stream of consciousness' in which memories and associations follow one another in quick and bewildering succession. The open stage dictated that actors either made long entrances across the wide stage or else remained immobile but continuously in view, as part of the action. Mielziner designed a large, craggy, free-form setting which could provide acting areas for individual scenes or a series of 'niches' from which the various characters from Quentin's past could assail the protagonist. Centrally located at the back of the set was a realistic concentration-camp tower which brooded symbolically over the entire play.

Kazan's direction, characteristically, drew from the actors vividly, realistic and emotionally true performances. In the case of the newcomer Barbara Loden, who played Maggie, this realism was distracting. Her performance amounted almost to an impersonation of Marilyn Monroe which by drawing undue attention to the autobiographical basis of the play seriously distorted it. As Quentin, Jason Robards Jr gave a subtly varied performance which was widely praised. But even the accomplished Mr Robards was not able, on the sprawling open stage, to raise Quentin's private anguish to the level of universal drama. Consequently, while some critics such as Howard Taubman of the *New York Times* praised the work as an attempt to grapple with larger issues, too many of the spectators (and critics) saw very little in the play beyond its superficial relationship to Miller's private life.

The problems involved in staging the play were not solved until Zeffirelli devised an ingenious décor of concentric steel bars and black drapes for a production he directed in Italy. This setting, supplemented with an elaborate system of backstage lifts, made possible the instantaneous appearance or disappearance of characters in Quentin's memory. In this production a better balance was maintained between the psychological–philosophical anguish of the central character and the related (but essentially subordinate) themes of Maggie and the concentration camp.

While it is probably true (as Miller maintains) that the New York critics never discussed the themes he was dealing with in *After the Fall*, the fact is not altogether surprising. For the play makes quite extraordinary demands on its audience. Miller is here attempting to present the kind of psychological detail that may well be beyond the scope of drama, which in some respects is a relatively blunt instrument. The associations and cross-references in the text are frequently too subtle to be caught in a careful reading let alone a first viewing in a theatre. Furthermore, the absence of a strong narrative line deprives the play of what some critics believe to be drama's soul. Many spectators or readers find it difficult to determine exactly what is happening in the play, and why it is 'happening' when it does. At certain moments Quentin acts in an external world, speaking to a Listener, lighting a cigarette, moving in an objective time and space. At such times he exists in a temporal present with past and future chronologically fixed. But this 'objective' reality is shadowy. We do not see the Listener, nor do we hear his (her?) words although we can deduce from Quentin's responses what they must have been. Compared to *Death of a Salesman*, for example, the real world hardly exists in this play, as Quentin's memories constitute almost the entire 'action'.

If Miller has abandoned almost completely any attempt to create a realistic context for Quentin's subjective life, his dramatisation of that life seems sometimes baffling or inconsistent. For example, Quentin is sometimes a character in his own memories, sometimes a superego standing apart from those incidents. Similarly the other characters in the play are sometimes actors in the drama of the past, sometimes accusers in the dialectic of the present. A more disturbing problem has to do with Quentin's level of awareness. It is not at all clear how certain insights gained into his own actions in the past affect his memory of various characters in the present. His recollections of his early happiness with Maggie are curiously unclouded by his knowledge of what subsequently happened. In other words, the incidents in the play are only partly released from their continuum in time. The strict chronological treatment of some parts of the past seems sometimes at odds with the convention of a universal present in the speaker's memory.

A related problem is the whole question of sequence in the drama. Do 'events' in the play follow one another according to any understandable principle, and if so what is it? That part of Quentin which we see is poised between the external, public, social, objective world and his own internal, unexpressed, scarcely understood needs and desires. His quest (like that of so many of Miller's heroes) is to reconcile the one with the other, to square what people tell him with what he knows, to align what his eyes say he must believe with what in his heart he wants to believe. Here the difficulty for the reader, let alone the spectator, is formidable. While it is just possible to puzzle out a coherent line of action for the Listener based on Quentin's replies, it is extraordinarily difficult to comprehend the workings of Quentin's unconscious. When he is surprised or puzzled by the associations his unconscious makes, has he been repressing that knowledge? How do we determine how accurate Quentin's recollections are? When is he rationalising to avoid issues he cannot face? Is there genuine change at the end of the play, or will Quentin simply begin his habit of repression and rationalisation all over again? Questions like this indicate something of the complexity and range of what Miller has attempted in this play.

The core of *After the Fall* is Quentin's relationship with his second wife, Maggie, which is treated in a compressed but chronological way in the last two-thirds of the drama. Embroidered around this story are memories from Quentin's childhood and later life. The juxtaposition of similar events from different periods of his life allows Quentin to generalise about his own experience, and draw from it conclusions which he believes are applicable to all human existence. This leads him to see parallels that extend still further into universal myths that are the expression of mankind's experience as a whole. The pattern of the myth – in this case the loss of Eden – helps him to understand his own nature and the nature of man. Gradually Quentin's life comes to seem to him to be that of a modern Cain wandering in a spiritual wilderness. Unlike his biblical counterpart, Quentin has forgotten his own crime, and has only dim memories of existence in a paradise where he had no consciousness of himself, nor any knowledge of sex or of his separateness from others. In the course of the play he re-enacts in his own experience the 'fall' of his parents. He discovers his exile from Eden, his difference in nature from his brother, the destructive intoxication of sex, and finally his capacity for murder. His eyes have been opened, but he has barely the courage to go on living with the burden of his knowledge.

It is easier to describe the nature of Quentin's spiritual and psychological education than to identify the specific stages along the way. He begins as a deeply divided individual with a profound sense that he has become a 'stranger' to his life. He cannot recognise himself in his actions by which he means (or at least reveals) that the image that he has had of himself can no longer be squared with what he has observed about his impulses and actions. In this state of psychic disorientation he tries to reconcile what he knows with what he feels. Emotionally he has always thought of himself as someone special, an individual capable of realising extremely high standards of love, altruism and self-restraint. Intellectually he knows, and has known for a long time, that he has not always lived up to his own ideals. This has resulted in an acute sense of guilt and finally in the feelings of a pointlessness and unworthiness that have paralysed him prior to his visit to the Listener.

The problem with the play is that Quentin's progress from ignorance to awareness is by no means clearly charted. Nor is it always easy to know when Miller is being ironic. It is apparent from the context of the play as a whole, for example, that Quentin is deluded when he sees Maggie as a kind of innocent pagan saint, but the strength of his affirmation of sexuality when he first takes her to bed may leave the spectator temporarily puzzled. Similarly, it is too easy for the audience to become involved in the personal dialectics of the drama without realising that the other characters have no objective reality. The relative guilt or innocence of other figures (especially Louise and Maggie) is not really at issue. What is of concern is Quentin's changing attitude towards these figures in his past. He begins by blaming others, 'These goddamned women have injured me',[39] but ends accepting his own culpability.

The first half of the play, therefore, constitutes a kind of prelude. Psychologically it represents a somewhat reluctant skirting of issues. The figure of the dissolute, drug-sodden Maggie is repressed, and only memories of the carefree meetings before their marriage are allowed into Quentin's consciousness. A start has been made towards self-knowledge, but Quentin remains essentially bewildered – genuinely unable to admit his own guilt and seeking to find explanations for his life in external causes. A concomitant of Quentin's inability to accept his own fallen nature is his continuing faith in moral absolutes. The failures of his mother, Mickey, Elsie and Louise to live up to his ideal of connectedness and love do not, in his mind, invalidate the ideal. On the contrary, Quentin seems to feel that, although others have 'sinned', a state of innocence is attainable. The ending of the act is heavily ironic as Quentin reluctantly faces the memory of his dead wife, realising that sooner or later he will have to confront her accusations.

The second act begins with Quentin prepared to go more deeply into his own unconscious. 'I think I can be clearer now,' he says. 'I am bewildered by the death of love. And my responsibility for it.' The juxtaposition in his mind between the hopes he felt at the time of his marriage to Maggie and the sad destruction of those dreams has made him feel that he is incapable of love. His life seems to him to be little better than a treadmill on which he is doomed to repeat the mistakes of his past. As he contemplates entering into a new relationship with Holga his fear and guilt make him look back on his marriage with Maggie with self-recrimination. The relationship is shown cyclically from their first ecstatic intimacy to their last sterile embrace before Maggie's attempt at suicide. In the aftermath of shock and depression Quentin can see only his egotism in the affair and nothing of his love. The movement of the second half of the play takes Quentin from a sense of overwhelming guilt to one of acceptance and responsibility.

Quentin's present interpretation of his relationship with Maggie (as opposed to what he thought at the time) is that it was motivated entirely by a desire for power. Paradoxically, however, the power he wanted was the power to protect Maggie from her own unhappiness. Quentin's sense that he had such power is derived from that feeling of being special, 'a light in the world', that he has acquired from his mother. Quentin's bewilderment stems from his feeling that he cannot live up to his special status. In comparison to his brother Dan's genuine altruism, his own unselfish gestures seem fraudulent. The Listener tries to get him to see the love in his acts as well as the vanity, but so great is Quentin's sense of guilt, that he finds it difficult to regard his feelings for Maggie as anything but dishonest.

The supreme irony of their early attraction for one

another is that Quentin perceived Maggie's apparent lack of shame and natural sexuality as a kind of innocence. He believed (wrongly as it turned out) that he could be open with Maggie in a way he could not with Louise. She inspired in him a desire to 'live the truth', but he has trouble in determining what that truth is. He suspects subconsciously that his apparent altruism is either a desire for power or possibly a reaction to his feeling of having been betrayed by his mother as a boy. But the sense he once had of seeing himself clearly is gone, and he goes over and over his relationship with Maggie in an effort to sort out the love from the guilt or innocence.

The heart of Quentin's problem is his ambiguous attitude to sexuality. His temperament and training lead him to regard Maggie with 'contempt' and to be ashamed of his desire for her which he suspects is nothing but lust. Because of this he has to rationalise his behaviour; he finds a 'principle' to justify his going to bed, adopts a posture to excuse his selfishness. Even as he remembers his first intimacy with Maggie he cannot call it 'love', but defines it as 'living in good faith'. He admits he is not 'innocent' or 'good' (as those words are understood by his family), but claims that he is at last 'saying yes to a truth'. In this sequence it seems clear that Miller sees Maggie as a kind of apotheosis of pagan sensuality, an identification which is made even more strongly in the TV version where Maggie is compared to Venus who 'knows the worst and the best . . . swallows it all like the sea, and it all becomes beautiful.'[40] But Quentin's attempt to embrace paganism is doomed from the start. Even at the climax of physical love he is conscious that the 'truth' he wishes to celebrate is unspeakable, contemptible, covered with slime, blind and ignorant. But whether Quentin is here recalling how he actually felt at the time he was making love to Maggie, or whether he is distorting the past because his bitterness makes him cheapen the truth, seems impossible to determine. All we can say for certain is that Quentin's attempt to escape from the world of intellectual abstractions by plunging into the world of blind sensuality failed miserably. And the climax of the play records the nature of that failure.

Because Quentin is secretly ashamed of Maggie, he unconsciously tries to change her while at the same time protesting that he adores her as she is. For a long time he believes that his love can reconcile their differences, but ironically and inexorably those differences kill his love. Maggie's demands on his time and nervous energy first affect the spontaneity of their relationship. As their sexual life deteriorates, it becomes evident that Quentin is more emotionally attached to his daughter than he is to his wife. Quentin believes that he can remain loyal out of a sense of duty, but gradually he realises that even loyalty is limited and, in the end, self-preservation takes precedence over all else. The cycle ends where it begins, in Maggie's bed. But in this last embrace there is nothing but self-disgust on Quentin's part. Not even Maggie's appeal to his 'humanness' can rouse the pity which was once the feeling that allowed him to overcome his shame.

When Quentin is brought to realise that he is a separate person, that he is not capable of limitless love, that in certain circumstances he might even be brought to commit murder, he must face what to him is the ultimate horror – that his most profound beliefs about the world and his own nature have been false. Contrary to what he had thought, neither socialism nor love is a cure for man's potential for evil. Even more disillusioning, he has been forced to acknowledge that he is not special, that far from being the 'light' of his mother's expectations, he is just like everybody else.

Characteristically, Quentin's reaction to the knowledge that he is no better than other men is to conclude that he must be worse. The final movement of the play traces Quentin's emergence from the despair in which he finds himself at the beginning of the interview. Faced with the fact of his 'original sin', Quentin has in effect two choices. He can despair and choose the escape of suicide chosen by Lou and Maggie, or he can face the truth and go on living. In choosing the latter, Miller implies, Quentin does the harder thing.

There are many weaknesses in *After the Fall*, but not, it seems to me, as many as some critics and spectators have charged. The work has provoked an astonishing amount of hostility toward the playwright, and there are still some who have never forgiven Miller for what they consider to be the naked exploitation of his relationship with Marilyn Monroe and the tasteless strain of self-justification in the play. For many, the play's message seemed to be little more than the summation of the reviewer from *Time* magazine, 'When things get tough, find a new woman and start again.' This is clearly a monstrous distortion of the work. But that such critical confusion could arise is at least partly the fault of the playwright. The form in which Miller has chosen to express himself in *After the Fall* is cumbersome and excessively demanding. Drama conventionally presents an 'objective' view of reality which enables the audience to distance itself from the protagonist by comparing his actions with those of other characters around him. The hero's self-delusion and the author's ironic viewpoint can be conveyed by juxtaposition and contrast. In *After the Fall*, no such distancing devices exist. The play presents only Quentin's experience, and there are few unambiguous signposts to show where Miller's view as playwright diverges from Quentin's as protagonist. This difficulty is compounded, of course, by the disconcertingly autobiographical nature of the play. Consequently it is extraordinarily difficult for an audience, or even a careful reader, to achieve the kind of detachment from Quentin that is essential if we are to view the play as art and not as true confession. Unfortunately, too few of the critics who have written about *After the Fall* have overcome that difficulty.

The obstacles to easy comprehension presented by the formal peculiarities of the work are compounded by the nature of its content. The play is not only about ambivalence, bewilderment and self-deception, it is an attempt to dramatise those very mental and emotional phenomena. But just as a play about boring people must not bore, so a play about confused people should not confuse. Much has been made of the rather 'forensic' nature of Miller's work. The plays are full of references to judges, courts, lawyers, briefs, and the format of many of the dramas resembles that of a trial or court of enquiry. This often seems to reflect a judicial view of life on the part of the author, a view that not only tends to see all issues in terms of right and wrong, guilt or innocence, but also assumes that it is easy to see the difference between the two. In *After the Fall* that comfortable assurance is gone. Indeed the play is largely about the loss of faith in the very possibility of passing judgement. In a world in which everyone is guilty, it is senseless to speak of 'innocence'. The whole apparatus of dialectic distorts the truth. Reality (and especially subjective reality) cannot be divided into categories of black and white, bad and good. Love does not exclude selfishness, betrayal or even hate. Moral absolutes if they can exist at all are possible only in a fabled Eden.

9
The Price

Like most of Miller's plays, *The Price* is about an individual's confrontation with his past. It shows the gradual stripping away of habitual excuses and illusions until the protagonist comes face to face with truths he has been reluctant to admit. The device linking past and present, subjective and objective, in this play is the sale of the contents of a New York brownstone mansion scheduled for demolition. The solid, outsized furnishings which had been purchased in the 1920s now seem of dubious value and beauty. The inevitable disagreement between the dealer's assessment of what the furniture is worth and the family's feeling of what they should get for it underlines the subjective nature of value and truth.

Setting a price on antique furniture, however, is considerably simpler than evaluating a human life. By certain standards it would appear that Victor Franz is a failure – that he has been willing to settle for too little in the bargain he has made with life. In the arguments with his brother and his wife that constitute the major conflict in the play,

Victor confronts and refutes their criticisms. He accepts the price he has paid as a fair exchange for value received. That others disagree with his judgement no longer troubles him.

Miller's shift from representing the past entirely through the eyes of one character, as he did in *Salesman* and *After the Fall*, to showing it through the conflicting memories and attitudes of Victor and Walter Franz has certain strong advantages. It enables the audience to judge Victor more critically and to recognise the role that self-deception has played in his understanding of himself and the world around him. But it has made the exact nature of the past more shadowy. Motives, and even facts, are obscure, and it is difficult for the audience or reader to choose between the different interpretations of the two brothers. Indeed, it appears that Miller has deliberately exploited this ambiguity.

About the major facts of the story there is general agreement. The play takes place in the attic room to which Victor and his father had retired after the crash of 1929 had reduced the Franz family from prosperity to relative poverty. Presumably, the management of the family affairs had been put into the hands of a number of uncles who took over the ten-room brownstone mansion and arranged for the renting out of rooms. At an undetermined time not long after the loss of the family wealth, Mrs Franz also died and Walter left home to attend medical school. This left the younger brother, Victor (who would have been about twelve in 1929), and his father alone in a two-room apartment on the upper floor of the house. Here they lived together with all of the family furniture which they had unaccountably crowded into the attic with them. About 1934, Victor began university and shortly thereafter met Esther, his future wife. In 1936, at about nineteen, Victor felt that he could no longer finance his own education and support his father, and he went to his brother Walter, then in medical practice, and asked for a loan of $500. The loan was refused. Not feeling that he could abandon his responsibilities, Victor gave up his plan to become a doctor, joined the New York police force, and continued to support his father until the old man died in about 1959. Because of the resentment he felt towards his brother, Victor had never been able to communicate with him easily and the two drifted apart. Since it appeared that the proceeds from the sale of the family furniture should be divided, Walter put off disposing of it for sixteen years until the building was about to be torn down. Finally he tries unsuccessfully to reach his brother, then goes ahead and contacts a used-furniture dealer to come to the apartment to negotiate the sale of the estate.

When one tries to reconstruct the past in this way from the bits of exposition in the play, it is evident that several important pieces in the puzzle are missing. When, for example, were Esther and Victor married, and what was the connection between this decision and Victor's decision to give up university? How did Victor pay for his first years of higher education? Who owned the house in which Victor and his father lived, and who got the rent for the rest of the building? Such questions seem petty at first, but they are a consequence of Miller's method. The play is a continuation of the debate begun in earlier works such as *After the Fall* about the ethics of survival. When, the play seems to ask, is an individual justified in sacrificing his own interest for that of another person? The answer to the question as Miller has formulated it seems to have to do with the extent of the other's need. We cannot know if the price Victor paid to keep his father from ending up on the grass was too high unless we know first if it was a fair one. If, as Walter maintains, the same end could have been achieved by selling the furniture, dipping into the old man's savings, or even forcing him to go out to work, then the ethical dilemma raised is not a true one. Much of the power of the argument is weakened if there is no way to choose between contradictory interpretations of the facts. We are left with Victor's satisfaction with his actions, but no objective standard by which we might determine whether or not his sense of values corresponds with our own.

The ambiguities in the play are at least partly a result of Miller's deliberate refusal to equate human and monetary value. The function of money is to enable one to express one set of values in terms of another (family heirlooms translated into vacations and fur coats). But such comparisons are ultimately meaningless. It is rarely possible to effect such an exchange (Victor's lost career as a doctor for his actual life as a policeman, for example) so that the price paid depends very largely in such cases on subjective factors. Factors such as resentment, disappointment, guilt, determine what the furniture dealer Gregory Solomon calls one's 'point of view'. Where Miller seems to differ in this play from earlier ones is in his apparent refusal to champion one point of view as clearly superior to all others.

The action of the play proceeds in two movements which could be described as 'setting the price' and 'accepting it as fair'. Gregory Solomon arrives at the crowded attic and after considerable delay offers $1100 for the furniture. Just as Victor accepts Solomon's terms and has some of the money in his hand, his brother and wife walk in and begin questioning the appraiser's offer. The play ends with Victor taking the balance of the money to close the deal. In their responses to Solomon the three characters reveal their different natures: Victor trusting, naive, incapable of bargaining; Walter questioning, aggressive, unable to settle for the status quo; Esther caught between her love for her husband and her desire for more of the things that money can buy. Walter and Esther try to persuade Victor to go along with a dishonest but legal income tax dodge which would net them altogether about twelve times what Solomon had offered them. Faced with the opportunity, however, Victor cannot seize it and he begins to try to understand what separates him from his brother, and what he has really done with his life.

Each of the characters in *The Price* has reached a crisis which has precipitated an intense self-examination. In the course of the play Walter and Victor are made to confront facts which they had 'known' about their lives but never before dared to face. The catastrophe is the now familiar reaction to insight upon which Miller has focused in earlier plays. The action of the drama itself consists of the gradual peeling away of 'fantasies' until each of the characters is forced to look upon the truth. The characters not only interact with one another on a realistic level, but they also bear certain symbolic relationships to each other and to the central meaning of the play. The central figures, of course, are Victor and Walter who, as brothers, seem 'like two halves of the same guy',[41] but whose 'respective psychologies and moral values conflict at the heart of the social dilemma'. Victor and Walter might be Biff and Happy twenty years later. They are the archetypal brothers we have come to know in several Miller plays – one selfish and materialistic, the other the radical idealist. Both brothers are a product of the crash and the Depression, but they have reacted to that catastrophe in opposite ways. The spectacle of his father's ruin inspired Walter with a kind of terror that haunted all his subsequent life. The fear of finding himself 'degraded and thrown down' as his father had been drove him to seek the kind of financial and social security that would render him untouchable. In the process he gave too little time to his wife and family, and lost them through divorce and alienation. Following a nervous breakdown Walter feels he understands what was the driving force at the root of his existence and has succeeded in living a slower-paced, more outgoing life since his recovery. Victor too has been shaped by the catastrophe that hit his family, but in a much more complex way. His perception that the world is merciless led him to reject the rat-race and to assert the importance of the human values of love, loyalty and human kindness. But a crisis somewhat like Walter's nervous breakdown was precipitated by his becoming eligible for a pension after twenty-five years in the police force. After a quarter of a century of planning a new life, Victor finds when the opportunity comes that he is unable to make a decision. He has begun to doubt that the values he chose as a young man are, in fact, as valid as he had believed them to be. Having started out believing that life was more important than the rat-race he has come to discover that there is no respect for anything but money. No longer sure what it was he was trying to accomplish, he looks back to see nothing but 'a long, brainless walk in the street'.

Part of the reason for Victor's uncertainty is his realisation that his dream of starting again in another career at fifty was an illusion. But he is also unsettled by his wife who has come to resent their poverty. Esther too had been forced to choose before she knew what was involved and now that their only son has left home for college, her relationship with Victor no longer seems enough to satisfy her. Not only has she started to drink, but envy of Walter's financial success is translated into dreams of a more secure life with Victor in a higher paid, more respected job. This vision is dependent, in her mind, on realising a substantial profit on the sale of the furniture, and Victor's refusal to accept Walter's offer of a job and money seems wilful and perverse to her. Her anger with her husband is prompted by his apparent surrender when the means for combat are at hand.

Central to the debate between Victor and Walter (and to Esther's final allegiance to her husband) is the question of clear-sightedness. 'What is the point?' Victor asks Solomon when the latter tells of his marriage at the age of seventy-five and the question lurks beneath the entire play. What is the 'truth' in any situation? Is it better to believe what you see or to invent yourself in order to act with conviction? There is no 'reason' for Gregory Solomon at age eighty-nine to continue working except that he loves it. There seemed to be no reason why the elder Franz should have given up when he lost his fortune except that he didn't have the heart to go on. More fundamentally, do the reasons for having done something in the past remain valid indefinitely? At the beginning of the play Victor is not sure. He says of his life 'I know all the reasons, and all the reasons, and all the reasons, and it ends up – nothing.' By the end of the play Victor's uncertainty is removed.

The heart of the drama is the searing confrontation between Victor and Walter which takes place in the second act. At the beginning of the argument each man is self-deluded. Walter has come to believe that Victor deliberately chose to become a policeman in order to avoid the rat-race (just as later Walter chose to work at a slower pace in order to give more time to his friends). This belief is based on his conviction that Victor could have financed his education if he had really wanted to. He comes ostensibly to tell Victor that he admires his courage, but really to assuage the unadmitted guilt he feels for having refused to lend Victor the $500 he needed to finish his degree.

Victor claims to believe that Walter owes him nothing

and that his decision to stay and support his father was his own choice. It is clear, however, that he harbours a bitter resentment against his brother, whom he secretly blames for abandoning his responsibility. When Walter offers him a substantial cash settlement for the furniture and a job in the new hospital, it would seem that all of Victor's dreams could be realised. But something makes him hesitate. He cannot overcome the feeling that he is being bought off and refuses to let the issue drop.

He begins by disabusing Walter of the comforting notion that he chose to give up science. In his opinion he was forced to abandon college for economic reasons, the principal one being that his father needed financial support and Walter was paying only $5 a month to help out. Walter denies that their father really needed help, and says that Victor was exploited. The violence of Victor's reaction to this suggestion shows that it expresses his own secret opinion. But Victor can neither express exactly how he views the situation nor confess his real resentment, so it is Esther who brings up the subject of the loan. It is Walter's refusal to lend Victor the $500 he needed to complete his degree which is the real obstacle between them, and Walter tries to justify what he knows in his heart is unjustifiable. Victor realises that Walter is trying to make up for the past by offering him a job and money, but he also realises that time has made that impossible.

> You can't walk in with one splash and wash out twenty-eight years. There's a price people pay. I've paid it, it's all gone, I haven't got it any more. . . . This is where we are; now, right here, now.

Furthermore, he sees and resents the implication that his life has been a failure and his sacrifice needless. Walter betrays his own deep ambivalence by admitting that while he might admire the decision to forgo the rat-race, he cannot respect poverty. In his own eyes, he is offering to save Victor by giving him the money and opportunity which he refused twenty-eight years ago. When Victor returns to the accusation that Walter walked out on his responsibility, the elder brother reveals that their father in fact, had money in the bank all during the Depression. This revelation stuns Victor and makes him re-examine what he really 'knew' about his father during this period. It turns out to be more than he then or subsequently ever admitted. In response to the probing of his brother, Victor has to acknowledge that he suspected that his father did have money, but he was reluctant to challenge him. When Esther realises that Victor may have known his support was not needed, she can think of nothing but the sacrifices they have made:

> To stick us into a furnished room so you could send him part of your pay? Even after we were married, to go on sending him money? Put off having children, live like mice.

To Esther, the father seems nothing but a calculating liar and Victor an accessory because in his heart he knew the truth. Gradually Victor comes to see that his decision to stay with his father was not dictated by economic factors so much as by a psychological need. When he saw the unemployed men in the park and realised that there was no mercy in the world, he felt it necessary to make a gesture affirming love and loyalty to prove to his father that things were not falling apart. Walter presses in to remove even this last illusion by pointing out that there was never any love in the Franz household.

There was nothing here but a straight financial arrange-
ment. That's what was unbearable. And you proceeded
to wipe out what you saw. . . . We invent ourselves, Vic,
to wipe out what we know.

Walter claims that the two brothers escaped from the
same trap by different roads, and that their animosity is an
illusion. Victor is prepared to acknowledge the 'unreality'
of his hatred for Walter and to accept responsibility for his
own choices, but he wants Walter to do the same. And he
realises that Walter's offer of reconciliation has not been
made in good faith.

You came for the old handshake, didn't you! . . . And
you end up with the respect, the career, the money, and
the best of all, the thing that nobody else can tell you so
you'll believe it – that you're one hell of a guy and never
harmed anybody in your life!

Victor refuses to grant his forgiveness, not because he
harbours any resentment against Walter, but because he
realises that Walter must forgive himself. This Walter is
unable to do, because he cannot face his past. Like other
Miller characters, he sees the evil in his soul but looks
away. Consequently he leaves the apartment convinced
that Victor has 'sacrificed his life to vengeance', deliberately
giving up a medical career in order to make his brother feel
guilty.

The resolution of *The Price*, although conventionally
moral, offers little consolation or inducement to virtue.
Victor and Walter remain unreconciled and we are not
intended, I think, to imagine much change in their outward
lives. Victor will not apply for his pension, but will

continue walking his beat. Walter in a very short time will be as busy and successful and rich as ever. The changes that have occurred are all internal. Victor has come to see that his support for his father was not forced upon him, but was an expression of his own nature and his love. 'I just didn't want him to end up on the grass and he didn't.' He also realises that he was foolish to have imagined that his sacrifice could have brought any reward, or sense of forgiveness. Virtue is its own reward. As for the worldly view that the price he has paid for his father's security is too high, that too is a matter of viewpoint. In the end Victor seems satisfied with the deal he has struck with his life. Walter's inner development is more difficult to measure. His response to the crisis of 1929 was selfish rather than altruistic, and consequently more awkward to justify in moral terms. It is clear that he is ashamed of his action and cannot accept his own guilt. If other Miller plays are a guide, we might expect him to flee from his conscience through suicide or drugs.

The play ends, not with any of the members of the Franz family, but with Gregory Solomon. Left alone with the furniture he is oppressed and worried by the challenge it presents. Almost distractedly he puts on the laughing record which Victor had played in the opening scene. Within minutes Solomon is reduced to helpless laughter and the curtain descends on his mirth.

The significance of this final action is ambiguous, and perhaps deliberately so. Without the benefit of the detailed stage directions an audience might well mistake Solomon's outburst for the laughter of triumph, the satisfaction of a successful dealer who has outwitted an honest client. Or it might be seen as an echo of the evasive laughter of the elder Franz when Victor asked him if he had money in the bank. I think it is almost certain, however, that Miller sees the laughter as a symbol of hope and courage, the qualities most necessary to overcome despair. For Solomon (as his name suggests) is not only the oldest, but also the wisest character in the play. And it is significant that the knowledge he brings has nothing to do with the themes of selfishness and altruism which have seemed to be central concerns of this play. Solomon's wisdom has to do with the more fundamental question of belief itself. What Miller seems to admire in Solomon is his realism. As Esther expresses it, he believes what he sees. He can look at the past without sentimentality or regret. He mourns the loss of his daughter who committed suicide, and he understands the implication that her death is in some ways his fault.

> I had a daughter . . . she took her own life. . . . But if it was a miracle and she came to life, what could I say to her?

Solomon's strength is not that he has found hope in some conventional creed, but that he can face life with courage. His daughter's suicide, we are told, was caused by her despair at losing her ability to believe in anything. Solomon says to Victor,

> Let me give you a piece advice – it's not that you can't believe nothing, that's not so hard – it's that you still got to believe it. *That's* hard. And if you can't do that my friend – you're a dead man!

In other words, it is easy to become disillusioned and see the world as meaningless. What is difficult is to see the meaninglessness and still act with hope. It is Solomon's ability to act in the midst of chaos that makes him a symbol of Miller's deepest convictions in this play.

The Price is one of Miller's most balanced achievements, a skilful amalgam of the playwright's principal themes and technical resources. At first glance it seems to be a return to the claustrophobic Ibsenism of *All My Sons*. But this is realism with a difference. The cluttered attic apartment bears a resemblance to such symbolic settings as the Eckdal attic in *The Wild Duck*, but it is more generalised in its application than most nineteenth-century symbolism. *The Price* shows the influence of contemporary dramatists such as Beckett, Ionesco and Pinter whose stage settings are often theatrical metaphors for the human condition itself. The Manhattan attic where Victor and his father lived is a symbol of an attempt to arrest time. The careful preservation of these remnants of a vanished prosperity reflect the inability of Victor or his father to give up the 'dream' the furniture represents. In its sad disarray, the room epitomises an ideal that collapsed with the stock market in 1929. On another level, the room evokes the metamorphosis of time. Furniture, clothing, records that had seemed beautiful in their time, now seem awkward or bizarre; and ideas and actions from the past suffer a comparable transformation. Confronted by the evidence of former feelings and actions, the characters find them incomprehensible. One's past is dead, like a daughter who committed suicide, and it is impossible to bring it back to life. The setting is as specific as the Keller backyard in *All My Sons* or the Salem of *The Crucible*, yet at the same time as universal in its implications as the placeless and timeless setting of *After the Fall*.

The action of the play also unites the universal and particular in an especially successful way. The Franz family shares the usual similarities with Miller's own. But the individuals comprising that family have been abstracted to enable Miller to focus on two concerns which have formed the core of his work. The framework of the action is provided by the two 'father' figures in the play. Mr Franz, dead sixteen years but still very much a presence in the play, epitomises defeat. Having espoused the values of free-enterprise capitalism, he could never recover when that system failed him. He is a close relative of Willy Loman. Diametrically opposed to Mr Franz is Gregory Solomon who seems to be the very spirit of life. Solomon has recovered after at least four depressions and gives every sign of being unstoppable. Not improbably these two figures embody something of Miller's own ambivalent attitude to life – his sympathy with the defeated and despairing, and his admiration for the courageous and hopeful.

The central characters, Victor and Walter, represent in an even more obvious way the conflicting sides of human nature that Miller has always been concerned with. These can be described as altruism and selfishness, socialism and capitalism, spiritualism and materialism. What sets his treatment of the Franz brothers ahead of his studies of the Keller or Loman brothers, or his comparison of Dan and Quentin, is his greater sympathy for the materialist. He now recognises that 'as the world now operates the qualities of both brothers are necessary'. Walter is the more conventional of the two brothers with his oppressive sense of guilt and his need for forgiveness. In earlier plays, Walter would have been the central character and the play would have focused on the nature and consequences of his antisocial behaviour. Typically the drama would have shown the purging of guilt through expiation (*Sons*), insight and expiation (*The Crucible*), blindness and expulsion (*View*). In *The Price*, Walter's story is not only subordinated to that of Victor, but it is left more or less unresolved. It is true that Walter too has paid a price for the abandonment of his responsibility to his father. He has divorced his wife, lost touch with his children, and suffered a nervous breakdown. But at the end of the play he claims to have overcome his sense of shame and to have exorcised his feelings of guilt. He will presumably return to his medical practice which has brought him not only wealth but considerable personal satisfaction. It may be that he will find no rest from the accusations of his conscience, but it is probably a little sanguine to think so.

No doubt Miller intends us to see Victor's story as something of a triumph, but the nature of his success is difficult for many to grasp. *The Price* is the most uncompromisingly moral of Miller's plays in that it rejects all the easy, and therefore popular, solutions. Virtue in *The Price* is not made attractive; it is given neither the sanction of martyrdom nor the blessings of prosperity. It has no reward but itself. True we are asked to believe that Victor walks out with a pure heart; but many will see his victory as hollow and catch in Solomon's laughter the justified derision of the flexible pragmatist for the stiff-necked idealist. Perhaps the most difficult lesson of this play is that there is no external arbiter of moral values. Each man must set his own price on his actions and then learn to accept his evaluation. This explains the disturbing ambiguity that many find in the ending. Viewed from the perspective of the average middle-class, moderately acquisitive spectator or reader, Victor is a fool who sacrifices a personal advantage for an abstract principle. His action and motives can hardly be understood in a society which has come to believe that value is a synonym for price.

10
'The Creation of the World and Other Business' and 'Playing for Time'

The Creation of the World and Other Business, which had a brief and unprofitable run in New York in 1972, is an interesting and complex play that deserves a chance to find an audience away from the intense financial pressures of Broadway. One cause of the perplexity which greeted this work is its unusual form and subject-matter. Having come to think of Miller as a realist, audiences were ill-prepared for the blend of whimsy and theology in this play reminiscent of medieval drama but of little since that time. In spite of its apparently novel form, however, *Creation* is closely related to Miller's other work. In this play the dramatist continues his exploration of the themes of free will, violence and responsibility with which he has been concerned since *After the Fall* and *Incident at Vichy*. It is, he says, 'the clearest expression of his religious beliefs that he's come to'.[42]

The play probes man's need for morality and the question of whether there is anything which makes our concepts of right and wrong inevitable. It centres on the conflict between God and Lucifer, but Miller's portrayal of these two figures is startlingly original and often puzzling. Lucifer at first seems to represent science or knowledge opposed to God's intuition and faith. Lucifer maintains that 'a thinning out of innocence' (by which he seems to mean 'ignorance') will lead to knowledge of the inner workings of nature and to increased wonder and praise. Later he argues that since Eve's pregnancy could not have been accomplished without his participation, he deserves some of the credit. He offers to take what he considers to be his rightful place at God's side as a 'corrective' to keep the world from impotent virtue. The enthroning of evil as a reality equal to goodness would, he maintains, eliminate guilt among men by removing the self-hatred which is its cause. If God could be seen to love even the Devil, then no one need fear His wrath. The wars and hatreds fuelled by a sense of absolute righteousness would come to an end making possible a second paradise on earth.

Against Lucifer's non-evaluative approach to morality, God opposes His own very subjective response. His distinction between good and evil is not a logical, but an emotional one. God cannot share His position with Lucifer because He does not love him. What Miller seems to be suggesting is that while love is perhaps the most God-like of human qualities, it is nevertheless limited, irrational and even dangerous.

A second important theme in the play is the nature and function of creativity. Like Shaw, Miller equates creativity in certain ways with the primal urge of life itself. Here too God and Lucifer are opposed – God the instinctive creator, Lucifer the rational critic. But the function of creativity is even more interestingly contrasted in the characters of Adam and Eve. Once outside Eden, Adam and Eve begin to discover the profound differences between their two natures. The most startling discovery is that, contrary to Adam's expectations, God has chosen to multiply mankind through Eve. While this might seem on the surface to be a mark of His favour, it is in reality the most glaring illustration of the irrationality of the world. For in the universe outside of Eden, it is the hungriest bird who sings best, the most violent act which appears most majestical. In such an inverted order, childbirth is at once the most privileged, the most creative, the most divine of acts, as well as the most cruelly painful. Not unreasonably, there-fore, Eve feels that God's curse is entirely on her, and she finds herself instinctively drawn more to the logical counsel of Lucifer than to the inscrutable will of God. At the moment of delivery, however, she is caught up in a feeling of oneness with God. Taking His hand she exclaims:

> I am the river abounding in fish,
> I am the summer sun arousing the bee,
> As the rising moon is held in her place
> By Thine everlasting mind, so am I held
> In Thine esteem.[43]

In a feeling of exultation God sweeps Eve away in a dance which is the purest and most joyous moment of communion between the human and the divine in the play.

Compared to Eve, Adam seems to be hopelessly bumbl-ing and ineffectual. He is shown as a traditionalist who clings to what he accepts as the rules of existence, and is at a loss without constant direction from a superior. He is far less practical than Eve, feels the loss of God's compan-ionship more keenly, and dreams continually of Paradise. If Adam is more 'otherworldly' than Eve, however, he does not seem to be possessed of those creative powers sometimes associated with otherworldly men.

Almost the only thing Adam and Eve have in common is their capacity for violence. Both parents at different times wish their unborn child dead although neither actually attempts to kill it. When Cain is born, he is declared by God to be innocent but imperilled by the evil in the world. Pointing to Cain, God tells Eve:

> Here is thine innocence returned to thee which thou so lightly cast away in Eden. Now protect him from the worm of thine own evil.

The development of Cain into a murderer proceeds in a series of stages that will be familiar to readers of Miller's plays. Cain's hatred of his brother is based on his conviction that he has been displaced. He senses (correctly) that Abel is his parents' favourite, and wonders why he has been given the backbreaking labour of tilling the earth while his brother need only tend the sheep. Cain's uncertainty about himself is increased when he becomes disillusioned with his parents. He first discovers that they were expelled from the garden; then he is shocked to learn of his parents' (and especially his mother's) sexuality.

> But you never said you were actually . . . *animals*. . . . God could never have wanted my mother going around without any clothes on!

The effect of this revelation on Cain is a heavy sense of guilt and a need to find the law that will define his nature.

> We've been living as though we were innocent. We've been living as though we were blessed: . . . if we will open up our sins to Him and cleanse ourselves, He might

show us His face and tell us how we are supposed to live.

Cain's search for meaning leads him first of all to wish for a return to innocence, and in the pursuit of that end to invent an elaborate ritual of sacrifice. The divine figure who first appears at Cain's altar, however, is not God but Lucifer, who proclaims a doctrine which seems to offer the innocence desired:

> A second time I come with thine awakening, Mankind!
> Nobody's guilty any more
> And for your progeny now and forever
> I declare one massive, eternal, continuous parole:
> From here on out there is no sin or innocence
> But only Man.

The religion of total freedom which Lucifer proclaims, although it seems at first to be a celebration of love, very quickly degenerates into an orgy of lust. When God appears, Lucifer proposes that mankind can be better served by a religion which offers two deities – one the God of what-men-are, and a second, the God of what-they-hope. Once again God declines to share his throne.

When God responds to the offerings on the altar, he does so in a completely subjective manner (choosing Abel's sacrifice because he likes lamb better than onions). Cain feels slighted and humiliated by the rejection of his offering, however, and in a fit of jealous rage kills Abel. When later he questions the 'justice' of God's choice, God replies in some surprise, 'When have I ever spoken that word?' He explains that his actions were a kind of test out of which he had hoped Cain would have emerged stronger;

How will [mankind] be shepherded as I have shepherded thee? Only if the eye of God opens in the heart of every man; only if each himself will choose the way of life, not death. For otherwise you go as beasts, locked up in the darkness of their nature.

Confronted by the murder of Abel, none of the survivors can admit a share in the crime. Eve blames God, Adam blames no one, and Cain knows no blame at all. In a fit of exasperation God offers to turn control of the world over to Lucifer. But Adam and Eve realise that a world in which there is no concept of guilt or responsibility is a world without love. The play ends with the couple reconciled with God, Lucifer still free to seduce mankind, and Cain condemned to wander the earth as the first alienated man, a fixed smile on his lips and anguish in his heart. God disappears into the stars leaving Eve as mystified as before. In the end it is Adam who makes the first halting step towards a solution. He realises that the only thing which separates man from the animals is his sense of responsibility, and that the prerequisites to understanding are love, forgiveness and mercy.

The Creation of the World is Miller's most explicit treatment of certain themes which are central to his work. What is significant about the play is that the conflicting forces (the way of life and the way of death) are here shown as complementary. Man's need for justice is no less compelling than his need for love, and yet, Miller seems to be saying, they are incompatible. Similarly, reason, curiosity and pleasure seem at times to be as admirable and as necessary as instinct, obedience and self-control at others. In the end, the contradictions in the world remain unresolved.

These contradictions are even more relentlessly explored in Miller's recent television drama, *Playing for Time*. In certain respects this work is simply an adaptation of the remarkable account by Fania Fénelon of her experiences in the women's orchestra at Auschwitz during the last months of the war. The original is a remarkable testament to a human being's capacity for endurance and hope, and as such it provided Miller with documentary proof of many of the things he has come to believe. Foremost among these is his conviction that man's need for a comprehensible explanation for the things that happen to him is as great as his need for food or sex. Fania Fénelon's ability to retain her dignity and humanity where others failed seemed to be closely related to her compulsion to understand. Her obsession that the apparent madness of the extermination camp *must* conceal some meaning led her to scrutinise her surroundings.

> I forced myself [to look at the prisoners]. I had to remember because later I would bear witness. This resolution was to harden and give me strength until the end.[44]

The longer perspective provided by her need to know gave her some kind of standard against which to measure the short-term compromises, and a weapon against the sense of hopelessness and despair that threatened to overwhelm her.

It is significant that the view of life that strengthens Fania Fénelon is not religious. It is based on a firm conviction of the importance of human solidarity, but it is leavened by a profound sense of irony. Her ability to feel passionately about things while at the same time being conscious of an underlying absurdity is very 'French'. It makes her conscious of the inconsistencies in human nature, and suspicious of generalisations. For this reason she is particularly hostile to fanaticism of any kind, and is able to see prejudice in the inmates at Auschwitz as well as in its jailers.

In his adaptation Miller has stuck very close to the original. He has simplified the secondary characters, making them slightly more representative of general types or attitudes, and he has followed hints in the source to soften the characters of some of the Nazis. There are, however, at least two ways in which Miller's version differs. It lacks the ironic humour, and it focuses more strongly on the paradoxical nature of art and the role of the artist in society. This is a subject to which Miller has given considerable attention but not, somewhat surprisingly, in his plays. To the young Miller, the artist was a kind of revolutionary prophet in whose hands art was a weapon for the abolishing of ignorance and the creating of a new, just state. But his early plays are indifferent or even hostile to the traditional arts. Characters who demonstrate any creative ability usually do so only in the practical arts such as cooking, dressmaking, gardening, farming or carpentry. Those attracted to the 'fine' arts (usually music) are shown to be effete outsiders (Rodolpho), neurotic (Maggie), or vaguely treacherous (Mrs Franz). Indeed the world of Miller's plays on the whole is as hostile to the artist as Puritan Salem. There are no painters, actors or dancers, and practically the only aesthetic pleasure recorded is the enjoyment of nature. Art is never an end in itself; so the 'writers' who appear in the plays are never poets, but rather lawyers preparing legal briefs.

Miller's apparently ambivalent attitude towards the arts suggests an extremely strong bias in favour of committed or engaged art, and something close to hostility for anything that might be called 'pure' art without any intellectual or social content. A similar bias seems to underlie his portrayal of Alma Rosé, the leader of the women's orchestra in *Playing for Time*. Whereas Fania agonises over the fact that their survival depends on their pleasing the Nazis with their music, Alma argues for the separation of art from its social and political context.

> What did it ever matter, the opinions of your audience? – or whether you approved their characters? . . . In this place, Fania . . . you will have to be an artist and only an artist. You will have to concentrate on one thing only – to create all the beauty you are capable of.[45]

In order to do this herself, Alma deliberately ignores what is happening around her. 'You seem to think that I fail to see', she says to Fania. 'But I *refuse* to see.'

Fania, by contrast, cannot separate art and life. In this she is shown to be rather a victim of forces beyond herself than an entirely free agent. This is suggested by Shmuel, a character Miller has introduced into the play. Shmuel, who is described as '*perhaps deranged, perhaps extraordinarily wise*', wanders in and out of the story bringing Fania news of the outside world and various timely admonishments. The earliest of these is a cryptic command to 'live' when Fania sees the resentment in the eyes of the prisoners not fortunate enough to be in the orchestra. The second is more ambiguous. After urging Fania not to look away from the horrors in the camp, he says, 'You have to look and see everything so you can tell him when it's over.' In response to Fania's puzzled question 'who?', Shmuel's eyes '*roll upward, and he dares to point upward just a bit with one finger.*' The suggestion that Shmuel represents some kind of otherworldly power is strongest at the end of the play when he brings news of the arrival of the British army. At that point, '*the light behind him contrasts with the murk within the building and he seems to blaze in an unearthly luminescence. He is staring in a sublime silence as now he lifts his arms in a wordless gesture of deliverance, his eyes filled with miracle.*'

Here Miller seems to be suggesting a new attitude towards the arts. On the one hand Fania is presented as a 'socially committed' artist who is celebrated in the play, not for her ability as a musician, but for her documentation of human courage and depravity. On the other hand, if the eye and mind to record what she sees are her own, the power to use them (or at least the will to use them) seems to come from outside. The nature of the otherworldly power that spurs Fania on is only hinted at. But it is possible that Miller is suggesting that its source is somehow in art itself. This may be the implication of the paradoxical presentation of Alma Rosé. For although Miller shows quite brutally that her music is powerless to alter the horrible realities of the camp or even humanise its guards, it is music that is the source of Alma's strength. And as blinkered as she is, it is Alma who is the strongest of the women, the one who saves them all by her 'refusal to despair'.

In *Playing for Time* Miller seems to have come to a new appreciation of the role of art. Here it is not the social function of music that is celebrated; the claim that music is humanising is seen to be specious. What is celebrated is the power of art to sustain the individual. In this respect the playwright has moved a considerable way from the position of his earlier plays.

11
Conclusion

Arthur Miller has spent most of his adult life trying to make sense of the events through which he and his contemporaries have passed. In his youth he absorbed from his environment a conviction that society could be changed, and that art could be an agent of that change. When he rose to prominence in the years just after the war, he tended to associate with similar-minded colleagues such as Harold Clurman, Elia Kazan, Kermit Bloomgarden, Mordecai Gorelik, Arthur Kennedy and Martin Ritt. He shared with such artists a rather idealistic view of drama based on the aims of the Group Theatre and the example of the plays of its principal playwright, Clifford Odets. He also believed that Broadway offered him his best opportunity to reach a wide cross-section of the public.

As his career proceeded, however, the financial pressures of Broadway began to split theatre-goers into more specialised groups. Increasingly the 'serious' public began to desert the expensive theatres for the more experimental, less lavish, productions Off-Broadway. For various reasons

Miller himself has never much enjoyed going to the theatre and perhaps for that reason his inspiration for formal experiment often comes from literary rather than theatrical sources (the dramatic classics or experimental prose works such as *The Fall* or *Hard Times* rather than The Living Theater). By the mid-1950s, therefore, Miller began to feel somewhat isolated, less and less able to communicate with the entertainment-seeking Broadway audiences and yet cut off from the newer experimental groups. Consequently he turned more and more to fiction and film.

The creation of the Repertory Theater of Lincoln Center seemed to promise the kind of theatre he had always hoped for. In its conception, the Repertory Theater was a revival of ideals of the 1930s, and as such may have been doomed from the beginning. By the 1960s, the establishment of a number of regional companies across the United States had radically altered the face of the American theatre. New York no longer constituted the only outlet for the American playwright. Many of the regional theatres were not only beginning to encourage new playwrights, but they could offer better conditions for the development of their work. The directors of the Repertory Theater of Lincoln Center hoped to duplicate those conditions – longer rehearsal periods, a resident company, opportunities for script development – in New York City. What they discovered, however, was what every high-minded theatre before them had discovered – that the only way to survive in the Broadway commercial environment is to behave like a Broadway commercial producer. The failure of the Repertory Theater to live up to its aims was more than a bitter blow to Miller. It was the death of a particular theatrical dream that had been in the air since the 1930s.

As conditions on Broadway changed, so did Miller's notions about playwriting. In his youth he had believed in the possibility of a kind of 'prophetic' theatre, and as late as the 50s was convinced that drama could 'raise the truth-consciousness of mankind' and 'transform' an audience.[46] 'I can no longer take with ultimate seriousness', he wrote in 1956,

> a drama of individual psychology written for its own sake, however full it may be of insight and precise observation. Time is moving; there is a world to make; a civilization to create.[47]

More recently, Miller seems to have moved away from the notion of the artist as prophet and closer to a conception of the playwright as photographer. Reflecting on his aesthetic theories in 1969, he maintained,

> I am not interested in making people grow in the sense I want to cure them of anything. Quite honestly I don't think I am motivated to do that. . . . One gets obsessed by certain images of reality and there is a certain beauty in putting them down within an aesthetic form.[48]

An individual's assessment of Miller as a playwright will depend, therefore, on his own biases and presuppositions. If he is primarily interested in theatrical experimentation and novelty, he will find little to interest him in the plays. Miller's explorations of form have never taken him far from the highroad of realism. The concept of 'pure' theatre – of a dance-like drama in which the meaning inheres in gesture, or of a circus-like drama of spectacle and acrobatics – has never appealed to the playwright. From the rich storehouse of theatrical trickery accumulated in this century by the expressionists, symbolists, surrealists or absurdists, Miller has borrowed practically nothing.

This is not to suggest that Miller has been indifferent to dramatic form. Quite the contrary. Indeed each new play has been a fresh attempt to find a suitable vehicle for his dramatic vision. When he has experimented with modernist techniques, however, it has always been in an effort to make his characters more psychologically real, never to render them mechanical, faceless or depersonalised. It has been to render the causal connections between things more understandable, not to suggest a world without meaning. To Miller, whatever their limitations, reason and language remain man's most reliable tools for understanding himself and his world, and attempts to discredit them or to substitute a 'poetry of the theatre' for poetry in the theatre have seemed misguided.

Miller's experiments with symbols, stylised or free-form settings, or choral figures to suggest a 'generalized significance' have not, on the whole, been particularly successful. Where he has made a significant contribution is in his creation of an effective stage speech combining the power of formal rhetoric with an impression of colloquial conversation. His most extreme experiment with deliberately heightened speech is *The Crucible* where the historical setting gives a certain licence for highly figurative dialogue. Miller's evocation of seventeenth-century language in this play has been much admired, but it seems to me less successful than his metamorphosis of contemporary American speech in several of his other works. Willy Loman's indignant or despairing outcries ('a man is not a piece of fruit' or 'the woods are burning') or Gregory Solomon's expostulations ('five hundred dollars they'll pay a lawyer to fight over a bookcase it's worth fifty cents') are random examples of the way in which Miller transmutes the idiom of the New York streets into something powerfully moving. Such approximations of the language really used by men seem to my mind greatly superior to the 'antique' locutions of *The Crucible* or the improbable rhetoric of Linda's 'Attention, attention must be finally paid.' Miller's best dialogue is that based on the slangy, wise-cracking speech of ill-educated or bilingual New York immigrants, mainly Jewish and Italian. Within this seemingly narrow compass of regional idiom the playwright expresses a remarkable range of feeling.

Miller's contribution to the development of a distinctively American stage rhetoric is important, but it is his attempts to extend the limits of conventional realism that will win him whatever reputation he achieves as an innovator. Miller once described his methods by saying 'I have worked in two veins. . . . In one the event is inside the brain and in the other the brain is inside the event. . . . That's why I've needed two kinds of stylistic attack.'[49] It is this symbiotic relationship between man and his social and intellectual environment that has always fascinated Miller, and he has gone further than any dramatist of his time in his exploration of the subjective on the stage. Earlier playwrights had used devices such as masks and soliloquies to reveal the unspoken thoughts of stage characters, but no one had dramatised the inner life of a character as Miller did in *Death of a Salesman*. The technique is commonplace now, but at that time it was so revolutionary that many potential backers (including producer Cheryl Crawford) found the play confusing. What is most novel is not the 'flashback' technique of dramatising events from the past so much as Miller's skilful interweaving of memory and reality. In this play Miller found a way to explode the chronological framework of conventional realism, and substitute for it the subjective reality of a continual present. It is precisely this ability of the brain to relate an event to a whole universe of memories, ideas, dreams and hopes that

Miller has always wanted to duplicate on stage.

As he found in *Death of a Salesman* (and still more in *After the Fall*), however, the 'stream of consciousness' drama has as many drawbacks as advantages. Among the former is the lack of accepted conventions that enable the playwright and the audience to set boundaries to the stage world. In the absence of some means of establishing 'objective' reality, there is a real danger that instead of suggesting a universal experience, a subjective play like *After the Fall* will seem no more than self-indulgent narcissism. Miller may yet return to the subjective form, but his formal experiments since 1964 have tended to focus on other means of generalising individual experience.

It is not the 'formalists' who are attracted to the work of Arthur Miller so much as the critics who continue to see in the drama one of man's most powerful means of exploring his own destiny. To such critics, Miller's determination to deal with the eternal themes of life, death and human purpose is one of his greatest virtues. But even Miller's admirers have not always been able to agree about the relative importance of various elements in his work.

Some see him primarily as a 'social dramatist'. Considered in this perspective, Miller is part of a tradition which descends from Ibsen through Shaw and the playwrights of the 1930s. Such dramatists, so the theory goes, present man in conflict with a repressive social environment. The underlying implications of their plays are that society is flawed, that the majority of men are too blind, superstitious or venial to see it, and that what is needed is a radical re-examination of conventional ideas in preparation for a complete overhauling of the system. Certainly *All My Sons The Crucible* and especially *An Enemy of the People* illustrate that these ideas do play a part in his work. But few of his plays are 'social' in the usual sense of that term. Their thrust does not seem to be outward towards the changing of political systems so much as inward towards the world of private relations and emotions. This has led some critics to describe Miller as essentially an observer of the family.

There is no question that one of Miller's greatest strengths is his penetrating insight into familial relationships. But to call him a dramatist of the family is also misleading if only because the range of his plays is surprisingly narrow. The typical Miller family consists of an ill-educated father, a mother with some cultural aspirations, and two sons. Sisters, grandparents and very young children hardly ever appear nor are their problems discussed. Furthermore, the families are almost invariably lower-middle-class. There are no 'movers and shakers' in the plays, and little concern with the problems of the 'rulers', whether these are considered to be politicians, scientists, engineers, financiers, or even writers and artists. The professional class is represented almost exclusively by lawyers, and the intellectual questions raised in the plays are discussed, for the most part, by non-intellectuals.

Even within this limited family unit it is only the men who are convincingly portrayed. It is one of the weaknesses of the plays as a whole that Miller fails to create believable women. The female characters in the plays are rarely shown except in their relationship to some man. They are not presented as individuals in their own right, but rather as mothers, wives or mistresses. The moral dilemma in a Miller play is almost invariably seen from a man's point of view, and to a large extent women exist outside the arena of real moral choice, because they are either too good (Linda, Beatrice, Catherine) or too bad (Abigail). They never experience the career or identity crises that affect men, nor are they shown having trouble relating to their parents or lovers. It is significant, too, that the obvious exceptions to this generalisation, Maggie and Fania Fénelon, are closely patterned on specific individuals.

Miller's tendency to see society as a 'home' and the family in terms of politics has led some critics to suggest that he should make up his mind which he is really interested in – sociology or psychoanalysis, politics or sex, Marx or Freud. But Miller never makes such distinctions. For him man is inescapably social ('the fish is in the water and the water is in the fish'), and it is impossible to understand an individual without understanding his society. What distinguishes Miller from some other 'social' dramatists is his recognition that the social environment is a support as well as a prison. Unlike Ibsen, for example, whom he otherwise resembles, Miller never shows self-realisation as a desirable end in itself. Selfishness in its various forms of materialism or self-indulgence is one of the cardinal sins in Miller's world. Man finds his highest good in association with others. On the other hand, that association must be voluntary, not coerced. Thus the other evil in the plays is an uncritical other-directedness (the handing over of conscience to others, or the pathetic desire to be thought well of by the neighbours). Miller focuses on the point of intersection between the inner and outer worlds, sometimes approaching it from one side, sometimes from the other.

It becomes apparent, I think, that in the final analysis Miller can best be described as a religious writer. He is not so much concerned with establishing utopias as with saving souls. This is why he is always more interested in the individual than the group. Systems – whether they be capitalism, socialism, McCarthyism or even Nazism – are not Miller's prime concern. They provide the fire in which the hero is tested. But it is not the nature of the precipitating crisis that interests Miller; it is the way in which the protagonist responds in that crisis. It is in this context that one can speak of 'sins' and indeed Miller sometimes seems almost medieval in his concern with such topics as conscience, presumption, despair and faith. Miller is quintessentially an explorer of the shadowy region between pride and guilt. His characters are a peculiar combination of insight and blindness, doubt and assertiveness, which makes them alternately confront and avoid their innermost selves. To the tangled pathways between self-criticism and self-justification there is probably no better guide.

Miller's heroes undoubtedly reflect many of the playwright's personal concerns. His entire career as a writer can be seen as an attempt to find justification for his own hope. In his youth he believed in the inevitability of socialism; later he sought salvation in personal relationships; in his most recent work he seems to have formulated for himself a kind of existential optimism. Miller's disillusion with an early faith and determined effort to find an acceptable substitute are in many ways the quintessential 'modern' experience. They can be duplicated repeatedly in the pages of literature from Wordsworth at the beginning of the nineteenth century through Tennyson, Carlyle, John Stuart Mill up to the present. Where Miller differs from many of his contemporaries, however, is in his guarded optimism in the face of the great mass of evidence that has accumulated in the twentieth century to undermine it. This is partly a matter of temperament, and partly because his experiences have been different from those of the European intellectuals who have been most articulate in their expressions of despair and nihilism. The Depression (the most formative crisis in Miller's life) was in many ways a positive force in that it often brought people together and elicited the best from individuals. The experiences of war, occupation and the Nazi terror (which were the nursery of existentialism and absurdism) tended to alienate people and bring out the worst in human nature. Miller's refusal to believe that man is a helpless victim of circumstances, therefore, is not so much his 'naiveté' as his exposure to different facts.

Miller is the spokesman for those who yearn for the comfortable certainty of a belief, but whose critical intelligence will not allow them to accept the consolations of traditional religions. What seems certain to ensure his continued popularity in a world grown weary of the defeatism of so much modern literature is his hopefulness. Like the Puritan theologians of old, Miller has come to realise that the greatest enemy to life is not doubt, but despair. And against despair, the individual has only faith and hope. In *Playing for Time* Miller presents the artist as the individual who refuses to avert his eyes from the horrors of the concentration camp in order that he may bear witness before heaven and mankind. It is Miller's chief merit as an artist that the evidence he presents in his plays seems, on the whole, more balanced than that of some of his contemporaries. If he has not hesitated to look on the evil in himself and in mankind, neither has he been willing to shut his eyes to the good.

References

1. 'A Propos of *After the Fall*', *World Theatre*, XIV (Jan.–Feb. 1965) 81.

2. Quoted in Richard I. Evans (ed.), *Psychology and Arthur Miller* (New York, 1969) 73.

3. 'The Shadows of the Gods', *Harper's*, CCXVII (Aug. 1958), reprinted in *The Theater Essays of Arthur Miller* (New York, 1978) 177.

4. 'University of Michigan', *Holiday*, XIV (Dec. 1953) 141.

5. Kenneth Rowe, *Write That Play* (New York, 1939) 52.

6. Jo Mielzinger, *Designing for the Theater* (New York, 1965) 23ff.

7. 'Journey to "The Crucible" ', *The New York Times* (8 Feb. 1953) II, 73.

8. *Psychology and Arthur Miller*, 72.

9. 'Introduction', *A View from the Bridge* (New York, 1961) vii.

10. 'Miller in London to See "Crucible" ', *The New*

York Times (24 Jan. 1965) 82.

11. 'Introduction', *Psychology and Arthur Miller*.

12. Quoted in *Congressional Record*, vol. cii, part 11, 14530.

13. Harold Clurman, *The Fervent Years* (London, 1946) 34.

14. Sam Smiley, *The Drama of Attack: Didactic Plays of the American Depression* (Columbia, Missouri, 1972) 59 and 75.

15. In Edwin Seaver, (ed.), *Cross-Section: A Collection of New American Writing* (New York, 1944) 517.

16. 'Introduction', *Arthur Miller's Collected Plays* (New York, 1957) 15.

17. *All My Sons* in *Collected Plays,* 124.

18. 'Introduction', *Collected Plays*, 19.

19. 'The *Salesman* has a Birthday', *The New York Times* (5 Feb. 1950) ii, 1, 3, reprinted in *Theater Essays*, 13.

20. *Psychology and Arthur Miller*, 23.

21. *Death of a Salesman* in *Collected Plays*, 148.

22. George Ross, '*Death of a Salesman* in the Original', *Commentary,* xi (Feb. 1951) 184–6, reprinted in Gerald Weales (ed.), *Death of a Salesman: Text and Criticism* (New York, 1977).

23. Marion Starkey, *The Devil in Massachusetts* (New York, 1949).

24. *The Crucible* in *Collected Plays*, 282.

25. 'Tragedy and the Common Man', *The New York Times* (27 Feb. 1949), and 'The Nature of Tragedy', *The New York Herald-Tribune* (27 Mar. 1949), reprinted in *Theater Essays*, 3–11.

26. '*A View from the Bridge*', *Theatre Arts*, xl (Sep. 1956) 62.

27. 'On Social Plays', reprinted in *Theater Essays*, 55.

28. Brooks Atkinson, 'A View from the Bridge', *The*

References

New York Times (9 Oct. 1955) ɪɪ, 1.

29. *A View from the Bridge* in *Collected Plays*, 437.

30. Sheila Huftel, *Arthur Miller: The Burning Glass* (New York, 1965) 161.

31. 'Introduction', *Collected Plays*, 52–3.

32. *Ibid.*, 53.

33. Quoted by James Feron, 'Miller in London to See "Crucible" ', *The New York Times* (24 Jan. 1965) 82.

34. *Situation Normal* (New York, 1944) 44.

35. *Focus* (New York, 1978) 184.

36. 'I Don't Need You Any More' (New York, 1967) 93.

37. *Ibid.*, 44–5.

38. 'The Misfits' (New York, 1961) 132.

39. *After the Fall* (New York, 1964) 6.

40. *After the Fall* (New York, 1974) 123.

41. *The Price* in *The Portable Arthur Miller* (New York, 1971) 438.

42. Tom Buckley, 'Miller Takes His Comedy Seriously', *The New York Times* (29 Aug. 1972)22.

43. *The Creation of the World and Other Business* (New York, 1973) 66.

44. *The Musicians of Auschwitz* (London, 1979) 54.

45. *Playing for Time* (New York, 1981) 73–4.

46. 'The Family in Modern Drama', *The Atlantic Monthly*, cxcvɪɪ (Apr. 1956), reprinted in *Theater Essays*, 84.

47. 'On Social Plays', in *Theater Essays*, 57.

48. *Psychology and Arthur Miller*, 34–5.

49. In an interview with Ronald Hayman in *Arthur Miller* (London, 1977) 14.

Bibliography

(i) Works by Arthur Miller

The Man Who Had All the Luck, in Edwin Seaver (ed.), *Cross-Section: A Collection of New American Writing* (New York: Fischer, 1944).

Situation Normal (New York: Reynal & Hitchcock, 1944).

Focus (New York: Reynal & Hitchcock, 1945; Harmondsworth: Penguin, 1978).

All My Sons (New York: Reynal & Hitchcock, 1947, and Viking: 1957; Harmondsworth: Penguin, 1961 [with *A View from the Bridge*]).

Death of a Salesman (New York: Viking, 1949, and Bantam, 1951; Harmondsworth: Penguin, 1961) and in Gerald Weales (ed.), Viking Critical Library Edition (New York: Viking, 1967; Harmondsworth: Penguin, 1977).

An Enemy of the People, adaptation (New York: Viking, 1951; Harmondsworth: Penguin, 1977).

The Crucible (New York: Viking, 1953; Harmondsworth: Penguin, 1968) and in Gerald Weales (ed.), Viking

Bibliography

Critical Library Edition (New York: Viking, 1971; Harmondsworth: Penguin, 1977).

A View from the Bridge, one-act version (New York: Viking, 1955) and in *Theatre Arts*, XL (Sep. 1956); two-act version (London: Cresset, 1957; New York: Compass, 1960 and Bantam, 1961; Harmondsworth: Penguin, 1961 [with *All My Sons*]).

Memory of Two Mondays (New York: Viking, 1955 [with *A View from the Bridge*]).

Arthur Miller's Collected Plays (New York: Viking, 1957; London: Cresset, 1958, and Secker & Warburg, 1974). Contains an introduction by the author and *All My Sons, Death of a Salesman, The Crucible, A Memory of Two Mondays*, and *A View from the Bridge*.

The Misfits (New York: Viking, 1961; Harmondsworth: Penguin, 1961).

After the Fall (New York: Viking, 1964, and Bantam, 1965; Harmondsworth: Penguin, 1968; New York: Bantam, 1974 [television adaptation]).

Incident at Vichy (New York: Viking, 1965, and Bantam, 1967).

I Don't Need You Any More (New York: Viking; London: Secker & Warburg; Harmondsworth: Penguin, 1967).

The Price (New York: Viking, 1968; Harmondsworth: Penguin, 1970).

In Russia (with Inge Morath) (New York: Viking, 1969).

The Portable Arthur Miller, Harold Clurman (ed.) (New York: Viking, 1971).

The Creation of the World and Other Business (New York: Viking, 1973).

In the Country (with Inge Morath) (New York: Viking, 1977).

The Theater Essays of Arthur Miller, Robert A. Martin (ed.) (New York: Viking, 1978).

Chinese Encounters (with Inge Morath) (New York: Far-
rar, Straus, Giroux, 1979).
Playing for Time (New York: Bantam, 1981).

(ii) Background and Criticism

HUFTEL, SHEILA, *Arthur Miller: The Burning Glass* (New
York: Citadel, 1965).

MOSS, LEONARD, *Arthur Miller* (New York: Twayne,
1967).

MURRAY, EDWARD, *Arthur Miller: Dramatist* (New York:
Ungar, 1967).

NELSON, BENJAMIN, *Arthur Miller: Portrait of a Playwright*
(London: Peter Owen, 1970).

WELLAND, DENNIS, *Miller: A Study of His Plays* (London:
Eyre Methuen, 1979).

CORRIGAN, ROBERT W, (ed.), *Arthur Miller: A Collection of
Critical Essays* (Englewood Cliffs, N. J.: Prentice-Hall,
1969).

EVANS, RICHARD I., *Psychology and Arthur Miller* (New
York: Dutton, 1969). An extended interview with
Miller.

CLURMAN, HAROLD, *The Fervent Years* (London: Dennis
Dobson, 1946). A history of the Group Theatre.

BENTLEY, ERIC, (ed.), *Thirty Years of Treason; Excerpts
from Hearings Before the House Committee on Un-
American Activities* (New York: Viking, *c.* 1971).

STARKEY, MARION, *The Devil in Massachusetts* (Garden
City, N.Y.: Doubleday, 1961).

GUILES, FRED L., *Norma Jean* (New York: McGraw-Hill,
1969).

GOODE, JAMES, *The Story of the Misfits* (Indianapolis:
Bobbs-Merrill, 1963).

Bibliography

MATTHEWS, JANE, *The Federal Theatre 1935–39* (Princeton University Press, 1967).

Index

Index